COMPUTERS, COMPUTERS, COMPUTERS

COMPUTERS, COMPUTERS, COMPUTERS

IN FICTION AND IN VERSE

D. VAN TASSEL, EDITOR

THOMAS NELSON INC., PUBLISHERS
Nashville   New York

Copyright © 1977 by Dennie L. Van Tassel

All rights reserved under International and Pan-American Conventions. Published by Thomas Nelson Inc., Publishers, and simultaneously in Don Mills, Ontario, by Thomas Nelson & Sons (Canada) Limited. Manufactured in the United States of America.

First edition

Library of Congress Cataloging in Publication Data

Main entry under title:

Computers, computers, computers!

    CONTENTS: Van Tassel, D. L.   Make way for the machines.—Brown, F. Answer.—Sandberg, R. T. The perfect crime. [etc.]
    1. Computers—Literary collections.
2. American literature—20th century.
I. Van Tassel, Dennie
PS509.C59C6   813'.5'4080356   77-2339
ISBN 0-8407-6542-8

ACKNOWLEDGMENTS

Glorobots by Gloria Maxson, copyright © 1975 by Technical Publishing Company, Greenwich, Connecticut. Reprinted by permission of *Datamation*.

Answer by Fredric Brown, copyright © 1954 by Fredric Brown for *Angels and Space Ships*. Reprinted by permission of Mrs. Elizabeth C. Brown and Agents for the Estate of Fredric Brown, Scott Meredith Literary Agency, Inc., 845 Third Avenue, New York, N.Y., 10022.

The Perfect Crime by Richard T. Sandberg, copyright © 1967 by *Data Processing Magazine*. Reprinted with permission from *Data Processing Magazine*, February, 1967.

Put Your Brains in Your Pocket by Arthur W. Hoppe, copyright © 1974 by Chronicle Publishing Company. Reprinted by permission of the author.

For Marge and Jim

CONTENTS

MAKE WAY FOR
THE MACHINES

Fear of being displaced is endemic in human beings, a haunting sword of Damocles from which no one quite escapes. Displaced in the affections of wife, parents, children. Displaced at one's job by someone more skilled. Displaced from one's home by a highway, a factory, an airport. Displaced in positions of public esteem, at sports championships, from honors of every sort. The King is dead, long live the King. Men are like streetcars—there's always another one coming along. No person is indispensable.

No wonder, then, that man is uneasy with the computers and cybernetic devices he has created. For the ultimate insult is to be displaced by a machine.

This theme, the role of the machine, is a common thread in science fiction. Sometimes the machine is evil, as in Barry Malzberg's "The Union Forever" or Fredric Brown's "Answer." Sometimes it is merely whimsical, as in Robert Heinlein's joke-playing computer in "That Dinkum Thinkum." Or it may be neutral and indifferent, as is Richard Sandberg's dispassionate dating computer in "The Perfect Crime."

Sometimes it takes semihuman form, as does Flo in Joseph Green's "Space to Move." Sometimes it teaches man an old, old lesson, like Barbara Paul's poetry-spouting giant brain in "Answer 'Affirmative' or 'Negative,' " Sometimes it learns a thing or two from irrational man, as do the electronic money system in Mack Reynolds' "Criminal in Utopia" and the intergalactic chess machines in Robert Sheckley's "Fool's Mate."

More often than not, the machine gets man into trouble out of sheer, perverse complexity. Consider the mess it presents to the electorate in Michael Shaara's "2066: Election Day." Or to the unfortunate Mr. Child in Gordon Dickson's "Computers Don't Argue." Or to Waldon Ashenfelter in Bob and Ray's tale of a man who can only identify someone he seeks by his name.

Here is a compendium of computers, presenting a broad array of views on man and machine by a variety of science fictioneers. In addition to the eleven short stories, there are comments from columnists Art Buchwald, Arthur Hoppe, and Jim Haynes, verse by Renn Zaphiropoulos, Laurence Lerner, and John Heath-Stubbs, and a collection of limericks by Gloria Maxson, which she calls Glorobots.

Are the computers going to take over? Well, people have different ideas about that.

DENNIE L. VAN TASSEL

COMPUTERS,
COMPUTERS,
COMPUTERS

The teacher's old influence fades
Since teaching machines became aides,
    And kiddies bring treats
    Of apples and sweets
To the robot computing the grades.

ANSWER

by Fredric Brown

Fredric Brown died in 1972 after a most notable career in science-fiction writing. Born in Cincinnati in 1906, he was educated at Hanover College, Indiana, then lived successively in Milwaukee, New York City, and Taos, New Mexico.

Starting out as a journalist and then a mystery writer (he won the Edgar Allan Poe award for his first novel, The Fabulous Clipjoint, in 1947), Mr. Brown turned to science fiction in the late 1930's. He has written about three hundred short stories and twenty-eight novels, both mysteries and science fiction, which have been translated into every major European language and read throughout the world. "Answer," the first story in the present anthology, is one of the most famous science-fiction tales ever written.

Dwar Ev ceremoniously soldered the final connection with gold. The eyes of a dozen television cameras watched him and the sub-ether bore through the universe a dozen pictures of what he was doing.

He straightened and nodded to Dwar Reyn, then moved to a position beside the switch that would complete the contact when he threw it. The switch that would connect, all at once, all of the monster computing machines of all the populated planets in the universe—ninety-six billion planets—into the supercircuit that would connect them all into one supercalculator, one cybernetics machine that would combine all the knowledge of all the galaxies.

Dwar Reyn spoke briefly to the watching and listening trillions. Then, after a moment's silence, he said, "Now, Dwar Ev."

Dwar Ev threw the switch. There was a mighty hum, the surge of power from ninety-six billion planets. Lights flashed and quieted along the miles-long panel.

Dwar Ev stepped back and drew a deep breath. "The honor of asking the first question is yours, Dwar Reyn."

"Thank you," said Dwar Reyn. "It shall be a question which no single cybernetics machine has been able to answer."

He turned to face the machine. "Is there a God?"

The mighty voice answered without hesitation, without the clicking of a single relay.

'Yes, *now* there is a God."

Sudden fear flashed on the face of Dwar Ev. He leaped to grab the switch.

A bolt of lightning from the cloudless sky struck him down and fused the switch shut.

Said a mellow old robot named Newman,
"When a man does not act with acumen,
But is clumsy and coarse
I consider the source,
And remember that he's only human."

THE PERFECT CRIME

by Richard T. Sandberg

Richard T. Sandberg is a graduate of the University of Min-
nesota and has studied computer programming and data pro-
cessing at UCLA. He lives in the Los Angeles area and writes a
story when his busy schedule allows it. "The Perfect Crime"
won a prize in a computer-related story contest.

Finding Alice by using a computer had been a stroke of genius. The idea had come to him when he saw an ad for a computer service that claimed to give scientific help in finding a mate. He hadn't really expected it to work at first, but now he had to admit that the results were exceeding all his expectations.

Of course, as far as he was concerned, it was basically a business proposition. What he had been after had been a woman with money whom he could subsequently separate from that money. He had done it before, and he had achieved a state of perfection through practice that left him with a sense of boredom. Finding out whether a computer could select for him a wife—"victim" would be a more precise word—better than he could do so himself added a spice of interest to this affair.

"I'm a man of substantial means. You have my permission to check my financial condition if you doubt that," he had told the man at the computer service. "Therefore, I don't want to risk being victimized by a gold digger. I want the woman you pair me with to have a substantial amount of money, too, so that the desire to acquire more will be eliminated as a motive on her part."

"I understand, sir," the man at the computer marriage service said. "Every effort will be made to accommodate you in that direction. However, the proper selection of a mate involves a detailed comparison of many traits of character and an analysis of how a pairing of those traits have resulted in the past in unsuccessful marriages. This is a task that can properly be accomplished only by a computer. That is why we ask each of our clients to take a psychological test, the results of which are stored in the computer's memory."

The test questions seemed straightforward enough, so he answered them as honestly as he could. After all, what did he have to hide? A liking for money and the things it would buy wasn't in itself reprehensible. If it were, all of us would have reason for shame to some extent. Besides, very few of the questions referred to money at all. They all seemed very innocuous.

It might be that the computer would select for him a wife with tastes the very opposite of his own. Maybe there was something to that old proverb that opposites attract. It was all very interesting. He did his best in filling out the questionnaire, more out of curiosity to see what type of woman he would be paired with than anything else. After all, the only thing that really mattered as far as he was concerned was the amount of money she possessed.

"I should warn you, Mr. Thomas," the man at the computer marriage service said, "that some of the questions aren't what they seem on the surface. The computer analyzes the questionnaire as a whole and sees subtle relationships between answers to apparently unrelated questions that wouldn't occur to a human analyst. So the questionnaire reveals far more about you than you might think."

Thomas still wasn't worried. After all, what did he have to hide?

A week later he was introduced to Alice Wyndham. "Miss Alice Wyndham, Mr. Robert Thomas," the man at the computer marriage service said. They nodded to each other and smiled. "Our computer paired you out of the more than two hundred million individuals in its memory. And it did so with a remarkable lack of hesitancy. We received no requests for additional information before the decision was made. This is a good sign of your complete compatibility and consequent chances for future happiness together. Good luck to both of you."

Alice turned out to be as innocent as a newborn babe as far as men and marriage were concerned. She had cared for an elderly mother until well into middle age. Her contacts with the opposite sex had been practically nil. Yet she was far from unattractive. When she was dressed up, she was even beautiful.

And she had other assets. She was a superb cook and an excellent housekeeper. She shared his interest in rare books and art. A gifted conversationalist, she enlivened his evenings at home.

Most important of all, she adored him. Her obvious devotion expanded his ego and mellowed his outlook on life. The large sum of money she had inherited seemed to become, incredibly enough, relatively unimportant. They were both really in love for the first time in their lives.

He concealed his previous marriages from her and passed himself off as a bachelor. In a sense, that was perfectly true because until then he had never really felt himself to be married.

Their enthusiasm for the ability of the computer to pair compatible people was sincere. "I really feel I'm a better person because I married you," he told her once. "I feel the same way," she said. "Tell you what, darling. Let's each will all of our money to a computer marriage service out of gratitude for what the computer did when it brought us together."

"I've got even a better idea, dear, and a more practical one," he said. "Let's each will all of his money to the other. The survivor then agrees to will all of the money to a computer marriage service. That way, whichever one of us survives will be taken care of, and a computer marriage service will get most of the money in the end anyway."

"Just what I would have suggested dear, if I were as practical and as perceptive as you."

Once the papers were drawn up, his usual hard, businesslike instincts came to the fore. After all, he had entered this marriage as a business proposition. It was no different from the others except that he had allowed himself to get soft-headed over Alice. True, this marriage had been particularly enjoyable, but now hundreds of thousands of dollars were within his grasp. Once Alice was gone, he would have the computer select another mate—one without money this time, so that he wouldn't be tempted again.

Getting her entire fortune willed to him had been incredibly easy. It had fallen into his lap, so to speak. Letting an opportunity like this go by, in spite of his affection for Alice, would be a crime. He smiled at her naïveté.

Now for the business of getting rid of her in a manner that wouldn't arouse suspicion, before he got soft-headed again. It had been an auto accident with Melinda and a fall while mountain climbing with Sally. About time for an accidental drowning, he would say. The insurance companies would be suspicious about so many claims, but they couldn't prove anything. The fact that he had willed her as much as she had willed him might help allay suspicions. Still, it might be well to avoid stretching his luck too far. Alice would definitely be the last. The money in her estate would satisfy him.

He wished he knew more about computers and had private access to one. Perhaps he'd be able to enlist its aid in planning the details of this most perfect crime. After the job it had done pairing Alice and himself, his confidence in its abilities was almost unlimited.

They arranged to spend their first anniversary at Lake

Tahoe. After doing a little gambling at Stateline, they'd rent a boat and spend a couple of days on the lake itself.

On the way north from Los Angeles, he almost changed his mind again. This woman had a pervasive charm that he almost couldn't resist. If only she didn't have so much money. But he managed to harden himself again. "Darling, we really know very little about each other even though we've been married for a year," she said at one point. "For all I know, you might be some sort of Bluebeard." His blood ran cold, but he managed to make his laughter at the joke sound unconcerned.

He gambled heavily at Stateline and lost. She was the one who pulled him away from the tables. He resolved that, when he had her money, he would study the applications of computers to gambling and even buy himself a small computer. But now to the business at hand. "No more gambling for me, darling," he told her. "Tomorrow we'll spend all day on the lake in the boat I've rented."

That night he made his way to the boathouse and made a small slit in the life preserver cushion she would be sitting on. It was small enough to look accidental and yet big enough to allow water to saturate the filling, making it sink gradually. Swimming was an accomplishment that Alice had not mastered. He attached a small charge to the bow that would make a hole that would look as though the boat had rammed into a partially submerged log.

She was asleep when he returned. Looking at her lovely, innocent face in the moonlight, he once more felt a momentary pang of regret. Then he slipped into bed beside her and was asleep himself in a few minutes.

The morning was bright and clear. A light breeze rippled the surface of the lake, which was otherwise disturbed by nothing except the wake of the boat. The odor of pine impregnated the air. He glanced at Alice. She was obviously ecstatic.

"You know, I think the reason I've been so happy with you during the past year is the fact that we enjoy doing so many of the same things together," he said.

"I've often thought the same thing," she said. "For example, you were the one who suggested coming up here for our anniversary, but there's nothing I would rather have done."

The charge went off prematurely, but no matter; they were far enough from shore, and the water was deep enough to accomplish his purpose. He was almost grateful that it had, because he felt he otherwise might have weakened enough to call the whole thing off.

She screamed when it happened. "Just a partially submerged log, dear," he said. "Looks like we've got an ugly gash in the bottom. But no need to panic. Your seat cushion is a life preserver. Just hold on to it until help comes."

"But I can't swim."

"I know, dear. The cushion will hold you above water. Don't worry about it."

A few minutes later, the boat had disappeared beneath the surface, and they were clinging to their seat cushions. The filling in hers would be slowly saturated with water until it dragged her under.

"Dear," Alice shouted from about a hundred yards away. "I have a confession to make."

What a uniquely appropriate time for a confession, he thought. "What is it, darling?"

"I really love you. I love you more than I've ever loved anyone else before. It was only your money that made me do it. I'm a weak person, and I just couldn't resist."

"What are you talking about?"

"I cut a hole in your cushion. In a few minutes, the filling will be saturated with water, and it'll drag you under. You see, I know you can't swim either. I didn't feel anything for John or Bill, but with you it was different. That's why I'm telling you this—so you'll know before you go under that I really did love you. I'm just a weak person. I'm so sorry."

"Are you crazy? I cut a hole in *your*—" He panicked as he felt the cushion begin to sink.

The computer had matched them so perfectly that even their weaknesses and homicidal tendencies were paired. He cursed and thrashed wildly, trying to keep himself on the surface. She paid no attention to him because she was likewise thrashing wildly and screaming, trying to keep her head above water.

In a few minutes, the surface of the lake was once again smooth, disturbed only by occasional bubbles.

> *A robot developed his skill*
> *At reading phonetically, till*
> > *He could say any word,*
> > *But the people who heard*
> *Could tell comprehension was nil.*

PUT YOUR BRAINS
IN YOUR POCKET

by Arthur W. Hoppe

Born in Honolulu and educated at Harvard, Arthur Hoppe has served on the staff of the San Francisco Chronicle since 1949, first as a reporter, later as a columnist. His astringent comments on every aspect of modern life have won him many devoted readers. He is the author of five books.

At last the American ideal of true equality for one and all is in sight. The harbinger is that latest rage, the pocket calculator.

In Berkeley, for example, the Board of Education has approved buying pocket calculators for tots who have difficulty learning to multiply. This way, they won't have to learn to multiply. Yet they'll be able to go forth and multiply perfectly for the rest of their lives—or at least until their batteries go dead.

The next step is obvious: a pocket computer with a miniaturized memory bank capable of storing billions of facts

23

and the ability not only to multiply but to analyze, deduce, and program solutions to every conceivable problem.

Actually, just such a device was developed as long ago as 1938 by the famed electronics wizard, Dr. Wolfgang von Houlihan. Realizing the tremendous potential for human equality inherent in his invention, Dr. von Houlihan decided to test it out first on his only son, Egbert.

Egbert was an ideal subject. It was not that he lacked the intelligence to do well in his school down the block. It was that he lacked the intelligence to *find* his school down the block.

But after weeks of patient instruction, his father was able to teach Egbert which buttons to push when. The change in him was startling.

With billions of facts at his fingertip, he naturally quit school. And, knowing everything, he naturally read nothing. And yet, unschooled and unread, he whizzed through life.

His employers were amazed by his incredible knowledge, his cool deductions, his brilliant analyses and his invariably perfect solutions. At thirty-five, he became head of General Conglomerated, Inc.

"I got my brains from my father," he would say modestly when complimented. And then he would hum a few bars of his favorite song, "I've Got a Pocketful of Brains."

His wit and erudition made him a hit at cocktail parties. He always said the right thing, did the right thing, voted for the right candidate and never ever once forgot his mother's birthday.

He was the perfect businessman, the perfect companion, the perfect citizen and—after he had computed the proper steps to sweep the beautiful Millicent Oleander off her feet—the perfect husband. While Millicent found Egbert singularly uncommunicative in the shower or in bed, she was perfectly happy with this perfect spouse who never ever once forgot their anniversary.

Needless to say, Egbert's father was overjoyed with the success of the experiment. "Just think," he cried. "When all people carry their brains in their pockets, all will be not only equal but perfect!"

Dr. von Houlihan was about to unveil his device for the perfection of mankind, when The Catastrophe struck. Afterward, he destroyed all his blueprints, muttering, "Equality's nice, but maybe we ought to just struggle along with what we've got."

What happened, of course, was that one morning while her husband was in the shower, Millicent sent his pants to the cleaners. And Egbert lost his mind.

GLOROBOT

NUMBER

4

Said a wild young robot, "Who's queasy
About mixing liquors? It's easy!
    Just take a racy
    Nip of the AC,
And then take a drag of the DC."

FOOL'S MATE

by Robert T. Sheckley

A New Yorker by birth and education, Robert Sheckley still lives and writes in his home town. He is the author of more than twenty science-fiction novels.

One of his favorite hobbies is playing chess—a passion he puts to work in "Fool's Mate."

The players met, on the great, timeless board of space. The glittering dots that were the pieces swam in their separate patterns. In that configuration at the beginning, even before the first move was made, the outcome of the game was determined.

Both players saw, and knew which had won. But they played on.

Because the game had to be played out.

"Nielson!"

Lieutenant Nielson sat in front of his gunfire board with an idyllic smile on his face. He didn't look up.

"Nielson!"

The lieutenant was looking at his fingers now, with the stare of a puzzled child.

"Nielson! Snap out of it!" General Branch loomed sternly over him. "Do you hear me, Lieutenant?"

Nielson shook his head dully. He started to look at his fingers again, then his gaze was caught by the glittering array of buttons on the gunfire panel.

"Pretty," he said.

General Branch stepped inside the cubicle, grabbed Nielson by the shoulders and shook him.

"Pretty things," Nielson said, gesturing at the panel. He smiled at Branch.

Margraves, second in command, stuck his head in the doorway. He still had sergeant's stripes on his sleeve, having been promoted to colonel only three days ago.

"Ed," he said, "the President's representative is here. Sneak visit."

"Wait a minute," Branch said, "I want to complete this inspection." He grinned sourly. It was one hell of an inspection when you went around finding how many sane men you had left.

"Do you hear me, Lieutenant?"

"Ten thousand ships," Nielson said. "Ten thousand ships—all gone!"

"I'm sorry," Branch said. He leaned forward and slapped him smartly across the face.

Lieutenant Nielson started to cry.

"Hey, Ed—what about that representative?"

At close range, Colonel Margrave's breath was a solid essence of whisky, but Branch didn't reprimand him. If you had a good officer left you didn't reprimand him, no matter what he did. Also, Branch approved of whisky. It was a good release, under the circumstances. Probably better than his own, he thought, glancing at his scarred knuckles.

"I'll be right with you. Nielson, can you understand me?"

"Yes, sir," the lieutenant said in a shaky voice. "I'm all right now, sir."

"Good," Branch said. "Can you stay on duty?"

"For a while," Nielson said. "But, sir—I'm not well. I can feel it."

"I know," Branch said. "You deserve a rest. But you're the only gun officer I've got left on this side of the ship. The rest are in the wards."

"I'll try, sir," Nielson said, looking at the gunfire panel again. "But I hear voices sometimes. I can't promise anything, sir."

"Ed," Margraves began again, "that representative—"

"Coming. Good boy, Nielson." The lieutenant didn't look up as Branch and Margraves left.

"I escorted him to the bridge," Margraves said, listing slightly to starboard as he walked. "Offered him a drink, but he didn't want one."

"All right," Branch said.

"He was bursting with questions," Margraves continued, chuckling to himself. "One of those earnest, tanned State Department men, out to win the war in five minutes flat. Very friendly boy. Wanted to know why I, personally, thought the fleet had been maneuvering in space for a year with no action."

"What did you tell him?"

"Said we were waiting for a consignment of zap guns," Margraves said. "I think he almost believed me. Then he started talking about logistics."

"Hm-m-m," Branch said. There was no telling what Margraves, half drunk, had told the representative. Not that it mattered. An official inquiry into the prosecution of the war had been due for a long time.

"I'm going to leave you here," Margraves said. "I've got some unfinished business to attend to."

"Right," Branch said, since it was all he could say. He knew that Margraves' unfinished business concerned a bottle.

He walked alone to the bridge.

The President's representative was looking at the huge location screen. It covered one entire wall, glowing with a slowly shifting pattern of dots. The thousands of green dots on the left represented the Earth fleet, separated by a black void from the orange of the enemy. As he watched, the fluid, three-dimensional front slowly changed. The armies of dots clustered, shifted, retreated, advanced, moving with hypnotic slowness.

But the black void remained between them. General Branch had been watching that sight for almost a year. As far as he was concerned, the screen was a luxury. He couldn't determine from it what was really happening. Only the CPC calculators could, and they didn't need it.

"How do you do, General Branch?" the President's representative said, coming forward and offering his hand. "My name's Richard Ellsner."

Branch shook hands, noticing that Margraves' description had been pretty good. The representative was no more than thirty. His tan looked strange, after a year of pallid faces.

"My credentials," Ellsner said, handing Branch a sheaf of papers. The general skimmed through them, noting Ellsner's authorization as Presidential Voice in Space. A high honor for so young a man.

"How are things on Earth?" Branch asked, just to say something. He ushered Ellsner to a chair, and sat down himself.

"Tight," Ellsner said, "We've been stripping the planet bare of radio-actives to keep your fleet operating. To say nothing of the tremendous cost of shipping food, oxygen, spare parts, and all the other equipment you need to keep a fleet this size in the field."

"I know," Branch murmured, his broad face expressionless.

"I'd like to start right in with the President's complaints," Ellsner said with an apologetic little laugh. "Just to get them off my chest."

"Go right ahead," Branch said.

"Now then," Ellsner began, consulting a pocket notebook, "you've had the fleet in space for eleven months and seven days. Is that right?"

"Yes."

"During that time there have been light engagements, but no actual hostilities. You—and the enemy commander—have been content, evidently, to sniff each other like discontented dogs."

"I wouldn't use that analogy," Branch said, conceiving an instant dislike for the young man. "But go on."

"I apologize. It was an unfortunate, though inevitable, comparison. Anyhow, there has been no battle, even though you have a numerical superiority. Is that correct?"

"Yes."

"And you know the maintenance of this fleet strains the resources of Earth. The President would like to know why battle has not been joined."

"I'd like to hear the rest of the complaints first," Branch said. He tightened his battered fists, but, with remarkable self-control, kept them at his sides.

"Very well. The morale factor. We keep getting reports from you on the incidence of combat fatigue—crack-up, in plain language. The figures are absurd! Thirty percent of your men seem to be under restraint. That's way out of line, even for a tense situation."

Branch didn't answer.

"To cut this short," Ellsner said, "I would like the answer to those questions. Then, I would like your assistance in negotiating a truce. This war was absurd to begin with. It was none of Earth's choosing. It seems to the President that, in view of the static situation, the enemy commander will be amenable to the idea."

Colonel Margraves staggered in, his face flushed. He had completed his unfinished business, adding another fourth to his half-drunk.

"What's this I hear about a truce?" he shouted.

Ellsner stared at him for a moment, then turned back to Branch.

"I suppose you will take care of this yourself. If you will contact the enemy commander, I will try to come to terms with him."

"They aren't interested," Branch said.

"How do you know?"

"I've tried. I've been trying to negotiate a truce for six months now. They want complete capitulation."

"But that's absurd," Ellsner said, shaking his head. "They have no bargaining point. The fleets are of approximately the same size. There have been no major engagements yet. How can they—"

"Easily," Margraves roared, walking up to the representative and peering truculently into his face.

"General. This man is drunk." Ellsner got to his feet.

"Of course, you little idiot! Don't you understand yet? *The war is lost!* Completely, irrevocably."

Ellsner turned angrily to Branch. The general sighed and stood up.

"That's right, Ellsner. The war is lost and every man in the fleet knows it. That's what's wrong with the morale. We're just hanging here, waiting to be blasted out of existence."

The fleets shifted and weaved. Thousands of dots floated in space, in twisted, random patterns.

Seemingly random.

The patterns interlocked, opened and closed. Dynamically, delicately balanced, each configuration was a planned move on a hundred-thousand-mile front. The opposing dots shifted to meet the exigencies of the new pattern.

Where was the advantage? To the unskilled eye, a chess game is a meaningless array of pieces and positions. But to the players—the game may be already won or lost.

The mechanical players who moved the thousands of dots knew who had won—and who had lost.

"Now let's all relax," Branch said soothingly. "Margraves, mix us a couple of drinks. I'll explain everything." The colonel moved to a well-stocked cabinet in a corner of the room.

"I'm waiting," Ellsner said.

"First, a review. Do you remember when the war was declared, two years ago? Both sides subscribed to the Holmstead pact, not to bomb home planets. A rendezvous was arranged in space, for the fleets to meet."

"That's ancient history," Ellsner said.

"It has a point. Earth's fleet blasted off, grouped and went to the rendezvous." Branch cleared his throat.

"Do you know the CPC's? The Configuration-Probability-Calculators? They're like chess players, enormously extended. They arrange the fleet in an optimum attack-defense pattern, based on the configuration of the opposing fleet. So the first pattern was set."

"I don't see the need—" Ellsner started, but Margraves, returning with the drinks, interrupted him.

"Wait, my boy. Soon there will be a blinding light."

"When the fleets met, the CPC's calculated the probabilities of attack. They found we'd lose approximately eighty-seven percent of our fleet, to sixty-five percent of the enemy's. If they attacked, they'd lose seventy-nine percent, to our sixty-four. That was the situation as it stood then. By extrapolation, their optimum attack pattern—at that time—would net them a forty-five percent loss. Ours would have given us a seventy-two percent loss."

"I don't know much about the CPC's," Ellsner confessed. "My field's psych." He sipped his drink, grimaced, and sipped again.

"Think of them as chess players," Branch said. "They can estimate the loss probabilities for an attack at any given point of time, in any pattern. They can extrapolate the probable moves of both sides.

"That's why battle wasn't joined when we first met. No commander is going to annihilate his entire fleet like that."

"Well then," Ellsner said, "why haven't you exploited your slight numerical superiority? Why haven't you gotten an advantage over them?"

"Ah!" Margraves cried, sipping his drink. "It comes, the light!"

"Let me put it in the form of an analogy," Branch said. "If you have two chess players of equally high skill, the game's end is determined when one of them gains an advantage. Once the advantage is there, there's nothing the other player can do, unless the first makes a mistake. If everything goes as it should, the game's end is predetermined. The turning point may come a few moves after the game starts, although the game itself could drag on for hours."

"And remember," Margraves broke in, "to the casual eye, there may be no apparent advantage. Not a piece may have been lost."

"That's what's happened here," Branch finished sadly. "The CPC units in both fleets are of maximum efficiency. But the enemy has an edge, which they are carefully exploiting. And there's nothing we can do about it."

"But how did this happen?" Ellsner asked. "Who slipped up?"

"The CPC's have inducted the cause of the failure," Branch said. "The end of the war was inherent *in our take-off formation*."

"What do you mean?" Ellsner said, setting down his drink.

"Just that. The configuration the fleet was in, light-years away from battle, before we had even contacted their fleet. When the two met, they had an infinitesimal advantage of position. That was enough. Enough for the CPC's, anyhow."

"If it's any consolation," Margraves put in, "it was a fifty-fifty chance. It could have just as well been us with the edge."

"I'll have to find out more about this," Ellsner said. "I don't understand it all yet."

Branch snarled: "The war's lost. What more do you want to know?"

Ellsner shook his head.

"Wilt snare me with predestination 'round," Margraves quoted, "and then impute my fall to sin?"

Lieutenant Nielson sat in front of the gunfire panel, his fingers interlocked. This was necessary, because Nielson had an almost overpowering desire to push the buttons.

The pretty buttons.

Then he swore, and sat on his hands. He had promised General Branch that he would carry on, and that was important. It was three days since he had seen the general, but he was determined to carry on. Resolutely he fixed his gaze on the gunfire dials.

Delicate indicators wavered and trembled. Dials measured distance, and adjusted aperture to range. The slender indicators rose and fell as the ship maneuvered, lifting toward the red line, but never quite reaching it.

The red line marked emergency. That was when he would start firing, when the little black arrow crossed the little red line.

He had been waiting almost a year now, for that little arrow. Little arrow. Little narrow. Little arrow. Little narrow.

Stop it.

That was when he would start firing.

Lieutenant Nielson lifted his hands into view and inspected his nails. Fastidiously he cleaned a bit of dirt out of one. He interlocked his fingers again, and looked at the pretty buttons, the black arrow, the red line.

He smiled to himself. He had promised the general. Only three days ago.

So he pretended not to hear what the buttons were whispering to him.

"The thing I don't see," Ellsner said, "is why you can't do something about the pattern? Retreat and regroup, for example?"

"I'll explain that," Margraves said. "It'll give Ed a chance for a drink. Come over here." He led Ellsner to an instrument panel. They had been showing Ellsner around the ship for three days, more to relieve their own tension than for any other reason. The last day had turned into a fairly prolonged drinking bout.

"Do you see this dial?" Margraves pointed to one. The instrument panel covered an area four feet wide by twenty feet long. The buttons and switches on it controlled the movements of the entire fleet.

"Notice the shaded area. That marks the safety limit. If we

use a forbidden configuration, the indicator goes over and all hell breaks loose."

"And what is a forbidden configuration?"

Margraves thought for a moment. "The forbidden configurations are those which would give the enemy an attack advantage. Or, to put it in another way, moves which change the attack-probability-loss picture sufficiently to warrant an attack."

"So you can move only within strict limits?" Ellsner asked, looking at the dial.

"That's right. Out of the infinite number of possible formations, we can use only a few, if we want to play safe. It's like chess. Say you'd like to put a sixth-row pawn in your opponent's back row. But it would take two moves to do it. And after you move to the seventh row, your opponent has a clear avenue, leading inevitably to checkmate.

"Of course, if the enemy advances too boldly the odds are changed again, and we attack."

"That's our only hope," General Branch said. "We're praying they do something wrong. The fleet is in readiness for instant attack, if our CPC shows that the enemy has overextended himself anywhere."

"And that's the reason for the crack-ups," Ellsner said. "Every man in the fleet on nerves' edge, waiting for a chance he's sure will never come. But having to wait anyhow. How long will this go on?"

"This moving and checking can go on for a little over two years," Branch said. "Then they will be in the optimum formation for attack, with a twenty-eight percent loss probability to our ninety-three. They'll have to attack then, or the probabilities will start to shift back in our favor."

"You poor devils," Ellsner said softly. "Waiting for a chance that's never going to come. Knowing you're going to be blasted out of space sooner or later."

"Oh, it's jolly," said Margraves, with an instinctive dislike for a civilian's sympathy.

Something buzzed on the switchboard, and Branch walked

over and plugged in a line. "Hello? Yes, yes. . . . All right, Williams. Right." He unplugged the line.

"Colonel Williams has had to lock his men in their rooms," Branch said. "That's the third this month. I'll have to get CPC to dope out a formation so we can take him out of the front." He walked to a side panel and started pushing buttons.

"And there it is," Margraves said. "What do you plan to do, Mr. Presidential Representative?"

The glittering dots shifted and deployed, advanced and retreated, always keeping a barrier of black space between them. The mechanical chess players watched every move, calculating its effect into the far future. Back and forth across the great chessboard the pieces moved.

The chess players worked dispassionately, knowing beforehand the outcome of the game. In their strictly ordered universe there was no possible fluctuation, no stupidity, no failure.

They moved. And knew. And moved.

"Oh, yes," Lieutenant Nielson said to the smiling room. "Oh, yes." And look at all the buttons, he thought, laughing to himself.

So stupid, Georgia.

Nielson accepted the deep blue of sanctity, draping it across his shoulders. Birdsong, somewhere.

Of course.

Three buttons red. He pushed them. Three buttons green. He pushed them. Four dials. Riverread.

"Oh-oh. Nielson's cracked."

"Three is for me," Nielson said, and touched his forehead with greatest stealth. Then he reached for the keyboard again. Unimaginable associations raced through his mind, produced by unaccountable stimuli.

"Better grab him. Watch out!"

Gentle hands surround me as I push two are brown for which is for mother, and one is high for all rest.

"Stop him from shooting off those guns!"
I am lifted into the air, I fly, I fly.

"Is there any hope for that man?" Ellsner asked, after they had locked Nielson is a ward.

"Who knows," Branch said. His broad face tightened; knots of muscle pushed out his cheeks. Suddenly he turned, shouted, and swung his fist wildly at the metal wall. After it hit, he grunted and grinned sheepishly.

"Silly, isn't it? Margraves drinks. I let off steam by hitting walls. Let's go eat."

The officers ate separate from the crew. Branch had found that some officers tended to get murdered by psychotic crewmen. It was best to keep them apart.

During the meal, Branch suddenly turned to Ellsner.

"Boy, I haven't told you the entire truth. I said this would go on for two years? Well, the men won't last that long. I don't know if I can hold this fleet together for two more weeks."

"What would you suggest?"

"I don't know," Branch said. He still refused to consider surrender, although he knew it was the only realistic answer.

"I'm not sure," Ellsner said, "but I think there may be a way out of your dilemma." The officers stopped eating and looked at him.

"Have you got some superweapons for us?" Margraves asked. "A disintegrator strapped to your chest?"

"I'm afraid not. But I think you've been so close to the situation that you don't see it in its true light. A case of the forest for the trees."

"Go on," Branch said, munching methodically on a piece of bread.

"Consider the universe as the CPC sees it. A world of strict causality. A logical, coherent universe. In this world, every effect has a cause. Every factor can be instantly accounted for.

"That's not a picture of the real world. There is no explanation for everything, really. The CPC is built to see a specialized universe, and to extrapolate on the basis of that."

"So," Margraves said, "what would you do?"

"Throw the world out of joint," Ellsner said. "Bring in uncertainty. Add a human factor that the machines can't calculate."

"How can you introduce uncertainty in a chess game?" Branch asked, interested in spite of himself.

"By sneezing at a crucial moment, perhaps. How could a machine calculate that?"

"It wouldn't have to. It would just classify it as extraneous noise, and ignore it."

"True." Ellsner thought for a moment. "This battle—how long will it take once the actual hostilities are begun?"

"About six minutes," Branch told him. "Plus or minus twenty seconds."

"That confirms an idea of mine," Ellsner said. "The chess-game analogy you use is faulty. There's no real comparison."

"It's a convenient way of thinking of it," Margraves said.

"But it's an untrue way of thinking of it. Checkmating a king can't be equated with destroying a fleet. Nor is the rest of the situation like chess. In chess you play by rules previously agreed upon by the players. In this game you can make up your own rules."

"This game had inherent rules of its own," Branch said.

"No," Ellsner said. "Only the CPC's have rules. How about this? Suppose you dispensed with the CPC's? Gave every commander his head, told him to attack on his own, with no pattern. What would happen?"

"It wouldn't work," Margraves told him. "The CPC can still total the picture, on the basis of the planning ability of the average human. More than that, they can handle the attack of a few thousand second-rate calculators—humans—with ease. It would be like shooting clay pigeons."

"But you've got to try something," Ellsner pleaded.

"Now wait a minute," Branch said. "You can spout theory all you want. I know what the CPC's tell me, and I believe them. I'm still in command of this fleet, and I'm not going to risk the lives in my command on some harebrained scheme."

"Harebrained schemes sometimes win wars," Ellsner said.

"They usually lose them."

"The war is lost already, by your own admission."

"I can still wait for them to make a mistake."

"Do you think it will come?"

"No."

"Well then?"

"I'm still going to wait."

The rest of the meal was completed in moody silence. Afterward, Ellsner went to his room.

"Well, Ed?" Margraves asked, unbuttoning his shirt.

"Well yourself," the general said. He lay down on his bed, trying not to think. It was too much. Logistics. Predetermined battles. The coming debacle. He considered slamming his fist against the wall, but decided against it. It was sprained already. He was going to sleep.

On the borderline between slumber and sleep, he heard a click.

The door!

Branch jumped out of bed and tried the knob. Then he threw himself against it.

Locked.

"General, please strap yourself down. We are attacking." It was Ellsner's voice, over the intercom.

"I looked over that keyboard of yours, sir, and found the magnetic doorlocks. Mighty handy in case of a mutiny, isn't it?"

"You idiot!" Branch shouted. "You'll kill us all! That CPC—"

"I've disconnected our CPC," Ellsner said pleasantly. "I'm a pretty logical boy, and I think I know how a sneeze will bother them."

"He's mad," Margraves shouted to Branch. Together they threw themselves against the metal door.

Then they were thrown to the floor.

"All gunners—fire at will!" Ellsner broadcasted to the fleet.

The ship was in motion. The attack was underway!

The dots drifted together, crossing the no-man's-land of space.

They coalesced! Energy flared, and the battle was joined.

Six minutes, human time. Hours for the electronically fast chess player. He checked his pieces for an instant, deducing the pattern of attack.

There was no pattern!

Half of the opposing chess player's pieces shot out into space, completely out of the battle. Whole flanks advanced, split, rejoined, wrenched forward, dissolved their formation, formed it again.

No pattern? There *had* to be a pattern. The chess player knew that everything had a pattern. It was just a question of finding it, of taking the moves already made and extrapolating to determine what the end was supposed to be.

The end was—chaos!

The dots swept in and out, shot away at right angles to the battle, checked and returned, meaninglessly.

What did it mean? the chess player asked himself with the calmness of metal. He waited for a recognizable configuration to emerge.

Watching dispassionately as his pieces were swept off the board.

"I'm letting you out of your room now," Ellsner called, "but don't try to stop me. I think I've won your battle."

The lock released. The two officers ran down the corridor to the bridge, determined to break Ellsner into little pieces.

Inside, they slowed down.

The screen showed the great mass of Earth dots sweeping over a scattering of enemy dots.

What stopped them, however, was Nielson, laughing, his hands sweeping over switches and buttons on the great master control board.

The CPC was droning the losses. "Earth—eighteen percent. Enemy—eighty-three. Eighty-four. Eighty-six. Earth, nineteen percent."

"Mate!" Ellsner shouted. He stood beside Nielson, a Stillson wrench clenched in his hand. "Lack of pattern. I gave their CPC something it couldn't handle. An attack with no apparent pattern. Meaningless configurations!"

"But what are they doing?" Branch asked, gesturing at the dwindling enemy dots.

"Still relying on their chess player," Ellsner said. "Still waiting for him to dope out the attack pattern in this madman's mind. Too much faith in machines, General. This man doesn't even know he's precipitating an attack.

. . . *And push three that's for dad on the olive tree I always wanted to two two two Danbury fair with buckle shoe brown all brown buttons down and in, sin, eight red for sin—*

"What's the wrench for?" Margraves asked.

"That?" Ellsner weighed it in his hand. "That's to turn off Nielson here, after the attack."

. . . *And five and love and black, all blacks, fair buttons in I remember when I was very young at all push five and there on the grass ouch—*

NUMBER

GLOROBOT

5

A robot who worked like a drone
Into deep melancholia was thrown,
And confessed in analysis
A sense of paralysis
Because his will wasn't his own.

POOLING INFORMATION
WITH A COMPUTER

by Art Buchwald

Readers have been smiling over Art Buchwald's acute observa-
tions on modern life since his column first started appearing in
the Paris edition of the New York Herald-Tribune and thence in
syndication around the world. Since 1962, his pearls of satire
have been cast from Washington, D. C., where he still lives.

Mr. Buchwald is the author of nearly two dozen books and
is in wide demand everywhere as a lecturer and commentator.

Somewhere in this great land of ours there is a computer
stashed full of information on you. Whenever you want
a bank loan, a credit card or a job, this computer will, in a
manner of seconds, give some total stranger almost every detail
of your life.

Unfortunately for most of us, the computer is unable to
discriminate between fact and malicious gossip, and once the
information is fed into it, it stays there forever.

43

The other day I was considering going into a car pool with three other men, Hicks, Kroll, and Anderson. I have known these men casually for years, but when you join a car pool, you really want to know what they're like.

So I asked a friend in the retail credit business if I could use his computer for a few hours.

He agreed and I went there and typed out: WHAT DO YOU KNOW ABOUT HICKS, AL, WHO LIVES AT 43 LOVER'S LEAP TERRACE?

The computer started chattering: HICKS, AL, BORN OCT. 23, 1925, BOTTLE-FED, BED-WETTER UNTIL 7 YEARS OLD.

I typed back: FORGET ABOUT CHILDHOOD AND GIVE ME SOME OTHER FACTS.

The computer replied: HICKS HAS A DOMINEERING WIFE WHO THE WHOLE WORLD THINKS IS SWEET AS MAPLE SYRUP. WHENEVER SHE GETS MAD AT HIM SHE STARTS BITING HIS NAILS.

I typed back: I'M NOT INTERESTED IN THAT. WHAT'S THE CONDITION OF HIS CAR?

The computer paused for a few seconds and then tapped out:

HICKS OWNS 1957 BUICK CONVERTIBLE FOR WHICH HE IS STILL PAYING $80 A MONTH. IT HAS BEEN IN THE GARAGE 33 TIMES AND HAS COST HIM $1,500 IN REPAIRS. TWO OF THE SPRINGS IN THE BACK SEAT ARE BROKEN AND HE NEEDS NEW SNOW TIRES. HE HAS THE CAR WASHED ONCE A MONTH.

It added: HICKS NEVER CHEATS ON HIS WIFE, THOUGH HE THINKS ABOUT IT A LOT.

THAT'S ENOUGH, I told the computer, NOW GIVE ME A RUNDOWN ON KROLL, H. G., WHO LIVES AT 1 LION'S DEN CIRCLE.

The tapes in the computer started turning furiously and finally stopped. The Teletype began to chatter: KROLL, H. G., HAD STRONG MOTHER WHO DRESSED HIM IN SILK SAILOR SUITS UNTIL HE WAS 13 YEARS OLD.

GET ON WITH IT, I typed impatiently.

HE OWNS 1970 FOUR-DOOR MERCURY SEDAN WHICH HAS SPECIAL SILK SEAT COVERS. LIKES TO DRESS UP IN HIS WIFE'S CLOTHES WHEN CHILDREN ARE AT CAMP.

THAT'S ENOUGH, I typed angrily. WHAT ABOUT ANDERSON, E. L., 198 DOVER CLIFFS?

ANDERSON IS HAVING A BIG THING WITH A LADY COSMETICS BUYER FROM LORD & TAYLOR.

WHAT ABOUT HIS CAR? I demanded.

THEY DON'T USE HIS CAR. THEY USE HERS.

I DIDN'T MEAN THAT. IS HIS AUTOMOBILE SAFE FOR OUR CAR POOL?

IT IS NOW. BUT IF MRS. ANDERSON EVER FINDS OUT ABOUT THE LADY BUYER . . .

THANK YOU VERY MUCH, I typed. YOU'VE BEEN MOST HELPFUL.

DON'T MENTION IT. OH, BY THE WAY, WHEN ARE YOU GOING TO STOP BEATING YOUR WIFE?

A man had a robot named Sadie,
Who was an impeccable lady,
Though unspeakable cads
Who described her in ads
As "cheap and fast" made her sound shady.

SPACE TO MOVE

by Joseph Green

A Floridian by birth and choice, Joseph Green can boast a long love affair with machines. In his time he has been a laboratory technician, a shop worker and welder, a construction millwright, a supervisor at Boeing, and an engineering writer.

Putting all this firsthand knowledge to work, he has authored a number of science-fiction novels and short stories.

"**K**en, I have received strong indications of an artifact ahead." The feminine voice of the ship's brain made the startling announcement in the same calm way she would have said his lunch was ready.

Jarred, Kenneth Williston raised his gaze from the special bio-instrumentation section on the pilot's console. He had been sampling the stream of data going into the computer banks. "What kind of artifact, Flo?" he asked the grille in front of him. "This is supposed to be a primitive planet."

"A large metal mass with the mixed spectros that indicate alloys, plus residual secondary radioactivity from anti-matter conversions. Almost certainly the wreckage of a spaceship. And yes, according to all the information in the memory banks no species on this planet approaches intelligence, with the possible exception of your vege-bird."

"The complete answer always," Ken murmured, in a low voice—but not low enough.

"My standing instructions are to answer all queries, even implied ones, as fully as possible," the grille responded immediately. "If you do not wish this service, please so indicate."

Ken leaned back in his chair, shaking his head in frustration. He should have learned by this time not to make sarcastic remarks to a disembodied brain. Aloud he said, "Sorry, Flo. Please keep feeding me all the pertinent facts, even the ones I may know. About this ship—can we land nearby, and is it safe to do so?"

"There is a clearing large enough for a vertical landing within sixty meters of the indicated center of metallic mass. The level of radioactivity is not dangerous."

"Fine; then let's go down for an explo."

"Heard and executing," the speaker in the console replied, with something of that distant coolness Flo managed to inject when she was offended.

Ken sighed, but not out loud. He had often wished, since starting this mandatory year in the field, that the university had furnished him a ship with a man's brain.

The trip ended with this planet, and it had been all he had expected. A tremendous amount of information was stored in the computer, enough to keep him busy analyzing it for centuries. It had been a fascinating experience. Now he understood why this lonesome year was a requirement for anyone seeking a doctorate in extraterrestrial physiology.

It had also been eleven months of an odd, strained relationship with Flo. He had always thought a human brain placed in a cybernetic machine lost its individuality, became little more than a complex biological computer. Now he knew that a great deal of the essential personality survived. Flo still seemed far too human to be considered only a part of the ship. It was more as if he had a living female companion, one he could not reach except through words. And somehow that was not enough. Over the months a subtle antagonism had developed, a challenge-response syndrome neither knew how to break.

The scout had been flying at two thousand meters, making an aerial survey while taking air samples. Flo took them down using only the antigravity generator, a silent, smooth approach. As the treetops neared she tilted the nose sharply upward and slowed, until the ship was barely drifting forward. Without being asked, she had fed a view of the landing site to the front viewscreen. Ken, tilted far back in his chair, watched as Flo extended the four pneumatic legs and settled gently through a gap in the trees. The ship came to rest with an impact the human pilot could barely feel.

The control and living quarters revolved to the horizontal position, and Ken unstrapped himself. The left viewscreen now showed the wreckage, a long, rectangular shape dimly visible in the tree shadows. It was partially overgrown with vines and creepers.

"Any danger outside, Flo?"

"There are no animals large enough to be a threat in the immediate vicinity. The air contains many spores of undetermined capabilities, and is thick with live bacteria. The use of the Protective Ensemble and vibra-filter seems indicated."

"Right; thanks."

Ken dressed in the PE suit with its heavy unibelt, then strapped the filter over his mouth. Two minutes later he was climbing down the ladder on the ship's third leg, taking deep breaths of the fresh, cool air of this Earthlike planet. The vibra-filter shook all microscopic bodies apart before they reached his face, and the hooded suit shielded head and body.

Ken approached the long bar-shape of the wreckage from the side, where an open crack led into the interior. He saw at once that this ship had been built by no species of which he knew, and that it had been here for centuries, if not millennia. It seemed an intruder in this green world of temperate forests and moderate undergrowth, an anachronism from the future somehow strayed into an Arcadian landscape.

As was his own 80-meter scout, towering above the tallest of the trees behind him.

Ken removed the powerlight from his unibelt, flashing it ahead as he eased between the jagged metal edges. He was in a large square room, filled with machinery he could not identify. He crossed between the tall racks to an open inner door, and through it into a corridor that apparently ran the length of the inhabited area. Ken started down it, toward what he judged to be the forward end.

"A large flock of the vege-birds is passing overhead at eighteen hundred meters, Ken," Flo's voice said over his suit radio.

"Thanks; we'll worry about them later," Ken replied, his eyes busy trying to take in all the small light disclosed. The builders of this harshly rectangular vessel had been functional-minded almost to an extreme. Even the walls of what was obviously the main passageway were lined with pipes, conduits, and cables. Compartment doors on both sides were mathematically spaced. After a little experimenting he learned how to open one, and flashed the light in several as he worked his way to the front. Most were jammed with equipment, some of it obviously portable in nature.

There were eight rooms apparently designed as living quarters just back of the bridge. Other than the fact that they were roughly his own size and humanoid, Ken could tell little about the former occupants' appearance.

A small camera fixed in the center of the unibelt had been automatically recording for the ship. As he reached the control room, Ken asked, "Flo, do we have anything in the banks that even remotely fits what we've seen here?"

"I've been feeding the pictorial data to the computer with a 'recognition' tag as it came in, Ken. So far there's been no response."

Ken opened a final door at the end of the long hall, and

found he had guessed correctly. Wherever these people were from, both their physiology and thought-patterns were similar to the human. The control room might have been an advanced design for one of the great liners that plied the starways between civilized worlds.

Ken was here for a detailed study of the little-known creature called the vegetable-bird, not a wrecked alien spaceship. But now that it had been found, he had no choice but to analyze and record all that he possibly could. The potential information gain was simply too high to be ignored.

Man was not alone in the galaxy, as he had often feared. Nevertheless, life-bearing worlds were rare, and those on which intelligence had developed rarer still. Only eight space-faring species had been located to date. Ken had lucked on to proof of the ninth.

"Ken, that flock of vege-birds I reported has landed in a tree about a kilometer away. They are feeding on fruit. This seems an excellent chance to attempt a capture with the Butterfly Boat. Shall I send it out?"

After thinking it over a moment Ken said, "Go ahead, but keep full active control yourself. If you are unable to capture one without physically harming it, stop the attempt."

"Understood. The boat is on its way."

The wreck was going to be here indefinitely; the vege-birds were not. Ken turned and hurriedly retraced his footsteps. He sped through the undergrowth to the tall spire of the scout, and climbed to the airlock. Two minutes later he was monitoring the attempted capture on his right viewscreen. This, after all, was his real business here.

As the anti-grav-powered Butterfly Boat approached the fruit tree, the alarmed vege-birds took flight. Their huge but thin green wings strained for purchase as they slowly flapped toward the safety of the upper air currents. Flo picked out a large adult and put the flying boat on its tail. Two long extendible metal arms moved upward from the main body and spread far apart; there was a fine-mesh net between them. The boat moved under and just ahead of the chosen specimen, until the net was almost touching its tail. The metal arms swung closed ahead of the flying bird, and it was suddenly a prisoner.

Ken watched carefully as the great wings were compressed by the metallic strands but saw no damage occurring. The collapsible arms retracted, drawing the bird inside the small flyer.

"Excellent!" Ken said. "Very careful work, Flo. Now as soon as we have it in a cage, make the usual external tests and see if one of our tranquilizers will be effective."

"Of course," the console speaker replied, in what seemed an injured voice.

Ken shrugged, and declined to apologize.

As the boat was returning he suddenly asked, "Flo, how much of the original you is here? I mean in the physiological sense."

"All of my brain, Ken, including the stem. Only the pineal and pituitary glands were removed."

Flo was extremely reticent when he ventured into personal territory, seldom volunteering more than the bare facts. And she flatly refused to speak of her past life; the memories seemed to be painful for her. She always operated the scout and its equipment with superb efficiency, but her attitude toward its pilot alternated from cold obedience to warm support. When in the latter mood she was often very helpful. But over their months together the coldness had come to dominate, as though she wished to have as little personal contact with him as possible.

Only persons dying young could specify that their brains be used in cybernetic machines; old heads were useless. But a living human brain, wired to a computer for memory storage and to slave controls for operational functions—such a brain entered a new and different form of life.

Flo could turn her sleep center on at will, or be alert for days at a time. Although her basic intelligence had not changed, she had immediate access to most of the computerized knowledge of mankind. Brains lucky enough to be chosen for starships saw with video eyes, felt with a hundred electronic senses the strange new worlds they found. The life might seem odd to a person in a healthy body—but it was far better, apparently, than no life at all. To date not a single cybernetic brain had asked to be turned off.

The Butterfly Boat reentered its compartment in the side of the ship, and Ken climbed down the central passageway to the lab. By the time he arrived, the vege-bird had been forced into the largest wall cage, which was just being extended into the room.

A whole battery of external instruments, from breath analyzers to electroencephalographs, hovered just outside the cage. After two minutes Flo spoke from a grille by the door. "Best indications are that two drugs are required for tranquilization, pure chlorpromazine for the animal tissue, zingjac for the vegetable. They should be compatible together. Shall I administer through inhalation?"

"No, wait a minute," Ken answered, holding up a hand— which he lowered when he remembered it was a useless gesture. He had been studying the vege-bird, and saw no signs of panic. It was, in fact, watching him!

Ken walked slowly across the lab toward the captive. Huge, protruding black eyes followed his progress. He paused a meter away from the cage; human and bird were almost at eye level.

The big eyes were set above a parrot's curving beak, on a head as round as a ball. The trunk was as large as his own, and covered with a thick gray down. Short, scale-covered legs were curled against the body. Even though folded, the wings were enormous, huge green curtains of very thin tissue stretched over a complex network of bone and cartilage. Overall the vege-bird made Ken think of some unbelievably outsized flyer from an unnatural union between bird and bat.

The truth was even more odd. This creature was a weird cross between animal and vegetable, the highest such form ever discovered. Those huge wings, five meters from tip to tip and almost two meters wide, were basically plant bioplasm supported by a bone framework. The cells contained chloroplasts, and when energized by sunlight the chlorophyll in them synthesized the usual carbohydrates from carbon dioxide and water. The body had most of the normal animal organs, plus two specialized ones that were more than half plant tissue. These transformed glucose produced by the wing cells into adenosine triphosphate, supplying the enormous energy required to live an airborne life. Normally the vege-birds stayed in the upper air currents, gliding through the daylight hours on wings spread wide to catch the sunlight. They both mated and gave birth to living young in the air. But they had to touch down occasionally and gorge on fruits, for the water and cellulose.

That much was known, and little else. A captured specimen had died on the way to Earth, and nothing could stop the fragile wings from decomposing. But the head had been thoroughly examined, and the brain inside was intriguingly large. Even in a rapidly expanding galaxy, where new wonders appeared every day, the vege-bird was a unique find.

The captive wings suddenly rose, tried to extend, began beating against the cage. The heavy beak struck at one of the bars, drew back, battered it again.

"Go ahead with the tranquilizer fog!" Ken called, hastily stepping back. Almost immediately a heavy vapor shot from an arm outside the cage, and a fan blew it around the struggling bird. After a moment it quieted. The dark eyes returned to Ken, watching him intently until they finally closed.

"Take some very small tissue samples from the wings," Ken ordered, and the mechanical arms moved toward the prostrate vege-bird . . . but paused.

Flo's mechanical voice, very low, said, "It's dead."

"It had to be the freedom-syndrome," Ken said, speaking loudly for Flo's benefit. "It wasn't the tranquilizer; this fellow just . . . decided to die."

"We have many similar instances on file," Flo agreed. She added, "I'm feeding a read-out on the tissue analysis to the lab station."

Ken was up to his elbows in gore, performing the dissection himself. He felt he learned more that way than by watching Flo's mechanical hands at work. He looked up as the printer clattered and produced a long sheet of paper, but declined to read it at the moment.

"Flo, this brain has an excellent storage capacity. All the sensory areas are highly developed. The input from the wing area alone is enormous."

"I've been checking your commentary against the data in the banks," Flo volunteered. "Virtually everything you've found is new."

"Good; that doctorate is practically mine," Ken said absently, probing after a major nerve trunk with the scalpel. He worked for another hour before his hands started shaking, and it was time to let Flo take over. She had video-recorded his part of the work, and would continue on her own.

Ken washed up and ate a late lunch. It was several hours before dark. He decided to return to the wreck and run a preliminary inventory. This time he took a large hand-held camera, and started at the rear. The engine room was sealed off. His instruments indicated the inside was too radioactive for safety, and Ken decided to leave that area alone.

In the third room on the left-hand side he found the ship's owners. There were eight sarcophagi, each one connected to an intricate network of tubing and electrical cable. The bodies inside were dried and withered, but not yet skeletons. Each head rested in a thick crystal helmet, out of which ran a maze of wires. As he had expected, they were almost human in appearance. A wider chest and heavier musculature indicated they originated on a slightly larger world.

But why suspended animation, when this was without doubt a faster-than-light ship? There was an easy, obvious answer that also explained why these aliens had not been encountered before. The distance to be covered was such that the travelers expected to spend many years in space, even at super-light speeds.

They were from another galaxy.

A little shaken, Ken went on with the prelim inventory. He finished in the control room again, and this time covered it in detail. Except for seven large odd crystalline structures whose purpose he could not define, he had seen similar control rooms on the interstellar ships of at least two species.

Ken examined the odd crystals closely. They were egg-shaped, as large as his torso, and rested on strong supports above flat-top cabinets. A cable as thick as his forearm fed into the bottom of each, and he could see thousands of tiny wires breaking out to unknown junctions. Above the base the interior became cloudy, as though filled with thin milk.

The thick cables from cabinets into crystals were covered with a peculiar sand-coated red tape. It looked familiar . . . and suddenly Ken turned and almost ran the length of the central corridor, to the room containing the eight sarcophagi. He found the identical cable he had noticed earlier, an abrasive, heavy red snake that emerged from an undecipherable tangle of wire and exited as part of a larger bundle leading to the main corridor. From there it continued to the engine room, and vanished through the fire wall.

Overwhelmed by what he had guessed, almost dazed, Ken stood as though partially stunned, staring at the mysterious cable . . . and Flo's voice in his earphone said, "Your heartbeat is too fast, and your sweat shows fatigue. Isn't it time for a rest?"

Ken pulled himself back from where imagination had taken him, and slowly turned to go. Flo was right; he had received about all he cared to absorb at the moment.

Outside, the sun was already down, and dark shadows filled the thick woods. Ken made his way through the undergrowth and up the ladder safely, but was barely conscious of his surroundings. Inside, as he stripped off the PE suit, Ken said, "You can stop searching the banks, Flo; there won't be anything on these people there."

"I have already confirmed that," Flo replied, in what seemed almost a tart tone.

Ken was still too awed to be annoyed. "It will take a little more work to be sure, Flo, but I think that ship is from another galaxy. I'd guess Ursa Minor, it being the closest to the Milky Way at this point. They had to enter a state of suspended animation to survive that many years. But . . . instead of having a computer operate the ship, they developed a way to transfer the mind—the *mind*, not the whole brain, a person's basic electrical pattern!—to the lattices inside a crystalline formation. My guess is that each of those seven electrically connected crystals held a mind that controlled some major part of the ship—and the cable I traced goes to an eighth one in the engine room!"

Flo was silent. Ken went on, "They were a big step ahead of us, and I don't quite know where all the implications lead. Can your mind become immortal in a crystal formation? Cybernetic brains age and die, like any others. Can we adapt their knowledge and move minds from body to body? And what is it like to lead a purely mental existence while connected to seven other minds, all of you together operating a complex machine like an interstellar ship?"

"I believe I can answer that last question with reasonable certainty," Flo said—and the tartness in her voice was now definite. "It doesn't matter if the minds are linked. Nothing—absolutely *nothing*!—can replace the loss of your senses. Any esthetic pleasure the mind can know is . . . pale and weak compared to sensual enjoyment. Check their procedures. I estimate an eighty-twenty probability they revived their bodies at regular intervals to live again for a while!"

Flo's unusual vehemence surprised Ken. "Perhaps," he said dubiously. "In any case, I know my first assignment tomorrow—to locate the machine that performs the actual transfer! It has to be somewhere in the wiring between the sarcophagi and the crystals."

Ken was right, and the particular machine proved easy to find. Most of the spaghetti tangle of wiring into which the red cable from the engine room dissolved led to a comparatively small cabinet in the next room. So did wires from each of the eight sarcophagi. From the cabinet, seven red cables ran to the crystals in the control room.

It was Ken's guess that the bodies were not reactivated until after the stresses of landing were over. But if that was correct . . . he investigated, and another piece of the puzzle clicked into place. One cable had been almost pulled out of the cabinet, snapping many connections. He traced it until it vanished into the engine room, and finished convinced that it was the power supply.

When the ship had cracked on landing, for whatever cause,

the bending of the long body had jerked the power cable out of the transfer machine. Possibly the smash-up had cut power to the control room as well. Regardless, the end result had been the inability of the minds in the crystals to reactivate their bodies.

Ken could only hope the ending for the imprisoned eight had been mercifully swift.

He spent the afternoon working on the major organs in the body of the vege-bird. The wings had started to decompose; so had the specialized organs containing plant tissue. The other internal organs were similar to those in many large ornithoids he had dissected. He excised the gonads last, and took samples for the analyzer.

Ken washed up and walked wearily to his bunk. He seemed to have barely closed his eyes when Flo was awakening him to the new day. Over breakfast he discussed the situation with her. Flo ran a logic check through the computer's memory banks, and agreed that the transfer machine, if they could restore it to an operational status, was probably the most important item on the wreck small enough to take home.

Flo had completed all the vege-bird tissue and fluid analyses while he slept, and informed Ken that nitrous oxide should be a harmless anesthetic for these giant flyers. They agreed that she would send out the Butterfly Boat again, and this time attempt to anesthetize the specimen while capturing it.

Ken returned to the wreck, and began the task of disconnecting the transfer machine. Fortunately, these far travelers had evolved a science and technology quite similar to the human. The eight primary input and output cables were installed by electrical connectors; only the power supply was a point-to-point contact. By noon he had it free. It was too large to pass through the crack in the hull, and he spent two more hours learning how to operate the manual controls on the single airlock. But before dark he had it outside, and on the scout's man-guided anti-grav sled. From there it was an easy trip to the lab.

Flo had also had a successful day. Awaiting Ken was a second vege-bird, this time a female. She was in the large cage, but unconscious.

It took Ken less than an hour, with help from Flo and the computer, to reconnect the torn wires from the power cable. A little experimenting was required to determine voltage and current, but he eventually found them. Intensive training in all the maintenance skills he might need were prerequisites for the use of a university ship. In another half-hour he had the box hooked up to ship's power, apparently ready to operate. He did not actually apply current. There was no way to be certain he would not damage the machine.

"All the knowledge on electrical equipment in the computer indicates you are safe, Ken," Flo volunteered. "It should operate as intended. But I have no correlates on function. The cybernetic-brain analogy is not close enough."

"It wouldn't be," Ken agreed. "We're forging into new territory. But I'd be tempted to try it, under controlled conditions back on Earth."

"I would try it now," said Flo, with the volume so low he barely heard her.

Ken jerked his head up, staring, as was his habit, at the grille where her voice originated. "Now what do you mean by that?"

There was a moment of silence, and then in measured, emotionless tones Flo said, "I have completed the physical analyses of the vege-bird brain, Ken. It is surprisingly complex for an animal, and even has small regions of higher thought. I think it might be possible to transfer my mind, minus certain of the abstract reasoning faculties, to the brain of this female in the cage."

For a moment Ken could only stare at the grille. Then he asked, "But why would you want to do that?"

"Why?" The mechanical voice rose, seemed to acquire emotion and resonance. "Why? Because I want my senses back! You can't know what it is like for me in here, Ken. Can you imagine being separated from your body? Are you aware that the memory can't *recall* sensory impressions? I know! I've spent a thousand quiet hours trying!"

Ken walked slowly to the cage, stood staring in at the long curved beak of the captive. Finally he said, "I was thinking yesterday, when I worked on the male's wings . . . there was a very rich network of nerves scattered throughout that thin membrane. I think . . . nature designed the vege-bird to take pleasure in the act of absorbing sunlight. There has to be a reason why they spend hours soaring with the wings extended, just riding the air currents."

"Yes, Ken, yes! I had already decided that. And today I saw two mating on the wing, from the airboat view-screen. The physical contact—seemed to last for hours, until the female had to move from under him, back into the sunlight. And when she gives birth . . . I had a baby by natural childbirth once, Ken. It hurt—you'll never know, no one who hasn't could know how much it hurt!—but it was a marvelous experience. I can't describe the emotions I felt even through the pain, you wouldn't understand, no man possibly could. And now . . . it's all gone. All that feeling of peace and rest afterward, the satisfaction, the sense of accomplishment—all gone. Just a cold intellectual memory, like something stored on tape. I lost it, Ken; it isn't a part of me any more! Can you understand? Do these words, into which I'm deliberately putting the inflections and emphasis and continuity breaks of passion, arouse an *emotion* in you? Then be glad; I don't feel a thing but an abstract longing. *I can't feel!* That's the crux of the matter, Ken. And I want to! I want to so much I'm going to be the first cyborg brain to ask to be turned off if I can't!"

Ken shook his head in frustration. The fury and torment in the voice might be simulated, a deliberate act, but to him it seemed real. He finally knew that most of Florence Kitchen's personality survived in the disembodied brain—and apparently the equivalent was true of all cyborgs.

"Look, we're taking this machine back to Earth," Ken pointed out. "Better qualifed scientists than you and I can analyze it, duplicate it, adapt it to our species. I'll take one of those giant crystals and its cabinet, too. In a few months, a year, you can make such a transfer safely and easily, perhaps into another *human* brain."

"There are no healthy human brains unoccupied, Ken."

"Then into an animal, if you want to reexperience sensory

input, one of the higher primates perhaps. Why risk killing yourself?"

"I can't think of any animal I'd rather be than a vege-bird, Ken."

"Because of what seems to be an unusually high capacity for sensuous enjoyment? We're only speculating, we can't know for certain that feeding on sunlight is such a voluptuous pleasure. As for the mating, other animals indulge for hours at a time also—including us! And besides, that bird has a poorly developed cerebral cortex, remember? Even if it worked you'd lose part of your personality, become something less than you are now. With all power of abstract reasoning gone, you wouldn't be a true human being any more."

"Am I now? I've thought of that, Ken. It's a harsh and dramatic choice, isn't it? I can remain pure intellect, cut off from all sensation and emotion, knowing the world around me only through the abstract of intelligence. Or I can force my mental pattern onto that bird, enough so that at least the basic person I am will survive, and regain my lost senses—and probably enjoy some new ones as well. But if I do, part of me must die."

Flo had reverted to her usual calm and somewhat distant manner, no longer injecting emotion into her voice. But her determination had not faltered an iota.

"I choose the latter course, Ken. If you deny me, then I will officially request my life support be turned off when we reach Earth. Believe me, Ken; I do not lie or bluff."

Ken slowly turned and walked toward the transfer machine. He said, "I believe you."

And he did.

Ken started removing the cover panel on the bottom of the cabinet. He had quite a job ahead if this transfer was to be accomplished safely. As he worked he suddenly threw back his head and laughed, then choked, and coughed. Some of that nitrous oxide Flo was blowing to the bird must have found its way to him.

Having no idea how long the vege-bird could survive without sunlight while dosed with anesthetic, Ken worked hard through the night. When the sun rose again he had done all he could. One crystal helmet and its wiring had been transferred from the wreck and reconnected to the input side of the cabinet. That had been the easy part, since he had connectors to work with. On the output side there had been only a tangle of wires that separated into the seven red cables. But Flo and the computer had confirmed his own best guess, that the larger crystals were similar to the small caps except in capacity. They were designed to contain a functioning consciousness, not merely transfer it. He had connected a second helmet into the output side.

"The computer gives us odds of sixty-forty based on what we've fed it, Ken. That's enough to satisfy me."

"I still think you should wait until we reach Earth. But having no emotions, you aren't capable of changing your mind, are you?"

"Do people reverse their convictions because of emotions, Ken? Although man prides himself on his reasoning faculty? I think you're right; it's a good insight. I'm incapable of changing my mind unless I receive new data."

"Then . . . I'll say good-bye while you can still speak, Flo. I'm ready to pull your braincase out of the computer."

"Good-bye, Ken. Ken . . . as much as any abstract and emotionless personality possibly can . . . I love you."

Ken choked again, and coughed, and cursed the gas from the cage that kept bothering him. In a strangled voice he muttered "Good-bye, darling!"—and almost ran for the computer.

The brain in its small case fit nicely into the crystal helmet. He slipped the other helmet around the head of the vege-bird without difficulty. And quickly, lest he should lose his nerve, he walked to the jury-rigged small control box and flipped the power switch.

White indicating crystals on the cabinet face lighted and flickered, then steadied. Ken hurried to it and pressed lightly on one metallic contact. There was a surge of power, a rising hum of energy that slowly climbed the tonal scale. The cabinet lights ran through a flickering repertoire of changing colors, the hum grew to a high whine—and just as it grew painful the sound died, and the lights faded back to the original pattern.

Whatever the machine had done, it was over. Ken hurried to the braincase. The small indicator at its base said that Flo, what remained of her, was dead.

Ken took charge of the manual controls and cut off the nitrous oxide. Hurriedly he opened the rear door of the cage, and operated the equipment to extend it into the air. A fresh morning breeze whipped through the opening and into the ship, bringing an early-morning smell of green and growing things. He had forgotten to activate the sonic barrier, and wasn't wearing the vibra-filter. He would have to decontaminate his body later.

The vege-bird stirred, raised a questing head. It gathered the short, weak legs under itself and staggered to the end of the cage, where it paused. There was no room to extend the huge wings. It braced itself, gathering strength. The round head turned, and protruding black eyes surveyed Ken with a look of . . . pity, or perhaps compassion, and maybe nothing at all. And then it launched itself into the air, falling fast as the great wings unfurled, slowing as they gained a purchase, then flapping once, twice . . . and near the ground it swung into a circle in the open space around the scout.

The wings beat strongly, the heavy body slowly rising, the buffeting sounds of compressed air coming clearly to Ken through the open hatch. *(What did it feel like to fly?)* The vege-bird circled the ship once, twice, and third time—and a few final flaps took it above the treetops. It climbed toward the sky at a gentle slant, and vanished from Ken's sight and hearing.

Ken retracted the cage and closed the hatch. Tired though he was, he walked to the pilot's console; he could sleep in space. "Run the automatic checks and then lift," he ordered the black grille in front of him. He waited . . . and there was no answer.

Slowly Ken lifted both hands, looked at them, then slid back the cover off a seldom-used portion of his console. Clumsily he began typing out his instructions to the computer, plotting a course for home.

Shrugged a robot with veiled defiance,
"One must display some compliance,
But though they adore me,
The humanities bore me,
My natural interest is science."

COMPUTERS
DON'T ARGUE

by Gordon R. Dickson

Gordon Dickson is a familiar name to all readers of science fiction, young and old. Since 1956, he has published nearly a book a year in both adult and young-adult fields.

Born in Edmonton, Alberta, Mr. Dickson served in the U. S. Army during World War II before completing his education at the University of Minnesota. He has won both Hugo and Nebula awards for his novels and, in addition to such long works, has authored more than 150 short stories, novelettes, and radio plays.

Treasure Book Club
PLEASE DO NOT FOLD, SPINDLE
OR MUTILATE THIS CARD

Mr. Walter A. Child   Balance: $4.98
Dear Customer: Enclosed is your latest book selection, "Kidnapped," by Robert Louis Stevenson.

437 Woodlawn Drive
Panduk, Michigan
Nov. 16, 1965

Treasure Book Club
1823 Mandy Street
Chicago, Illinois

Dear Sirs:

I wrote you recently about the computer punch card you sent, billing me for "Kim," by Rudyard Kipling. I did not open the package containing it until I had already mailed you my check for the amount on the card. On opening the package, I found the book missing half its pages. I sent it back to you, requesting either another copy or my money back. Instead, you have sent me a copy of "Kidnapped," by Robert Louis Stevenson. Will you please straighten this out?

I hereby return the copy of "Kidnapped."

Sincerely yours,
Walter A. Child

Treasure Book Club
SECOND NOTICE
PLEASE DO NOT FOLD, SPINDLE
OR MUTILATE THIS CARD

Mr. Walter A. Child   Balance: $4.98
For "Kidnapped," by Robert Louis Stevenson
(If remittance has been made for the above, please disregard this notice)

437 Woodlawn Drive
Panduk, Michigan
Jan. 21, 1966

Treasure Book Club
1823 Mandy Street
Chicago, Illinois

Dear Sirs:

May I direct your attention to my letter of November 16, 1965? You are still continuing to dun me with computer punch cards for a book I did not order. Whereas, actually, it is your company that owes me money.

Sincerely yours,
Walter A. Child

Treasure Book Club
1823 Mandy Street
Chicago, Illinois
Feb. 1, 1966

Mr. Walter A. Child
437 Woodlawn Drive
Panduk, Michigan

Dear Mr. Child:

We have sent you a number of reminders concerning an amount owing to us as a result of book purchases you have made from us. This amount, which is $4.98, is now long overdue.

This situation is disappointing to us, particularly since there was no hesitation on our part in extending you credit at the time original arrangements for these purchases were made by you. If we do not receive hayment in full by return mail, we will be forced to turn the matter over to a collection agency.

Very truly yours,
Samuel P. Grimes
Collection Manager

437 Woodlawn Drive
Panduk, Michigan
Feb. 5, 1966

Dear Mr. Grimes:

Will you stop sending me punch cards and form letters and make me some kind of a direct answer from a human being?

I don't owe you money. You owe me money. Maybe I should turn your company over to a collection agency.

Walter A. Child

FEDERAL COLLECTION OUTFIT

88 Prince Street
Chicago, Illinois
Feb. 28, 1966

Mr. Walter A. Child
437 Woodlawn Drive
Panduk, Michigan

Dear Mr. Child:

Your account with the Treasure Book Club, of $4.98 plus interest and charges, has been turned over to our agency for collection. The amount due is now $6.83. Please send your check for this amount or we shall be forced to take immediate action.

Jacob N. Harshe
Vice President

FEDERAL COLLECTION OUTFIT

88 Prince Street
Chicago, Illinois
April 8, 1966

Mr. Walter A. Child
437 Woodlawn Drive
Panduk, Michigan

Dear Mr. Child:

You have seen fit to ignore our courteous requests to settle your long overdue account with Treasure Book Club, which is now, with accumulated interest and charges, in the amount of $7.51.

If payment in full is not forthcoming by April 11, 1966, we will be forced to turn the matter over to our attorneys for immediate court action.

Ezekiel B. Harshe
President

MALONEY, MAHONEY,
MACNAMARA AND PRUITT
Attorneys

89 Prince Street
Chicago, Illinois
April 29, 1966

Mr. Walter A. Child
437 Woodlawn Drive
Panduk, Michigan

Dear Mr. Child:

Your indebtedness to the Treasure Book Club has been referred to us for legal action to collect.

This indebtedness is now in the amount of $10.01. If you will send us this amount so that we may receive it before May 5,

1966, the matter may be satisfied. However, if we do not receive satisfaction in full by that date, we will take steps to collect through the courts.

I am sure you will see the advantage of avoiding a judgment against you, which as a matter of record would do lasting harm to your credit rating.

Very truly yours,
Hagthorpe M. Pruitt, Jr.
Attorney at law

437 Woodlawn Drive
Panduk, Michigan
May 4, 1966

Mr. Hagthorpe M. Pruitt, Jr.
Maloney, Mahoney, MacNamara and Pruitt
89 Prince Street
Chicago, Illinois

Dear Mr. Pruitt:

You don't know what a pleasure it is to me in this matter to get a letter from a live human being to whom I can explain the situation.

This whole matter is silly. I explained it fully in my letters to the Treasure Book Company. But I might as well have been trying to explain to the computer that puts out their punch cards, for all the good it seemed to do. Briefly, what happened was I ordered a copy of "Kim," by Rudyard Kipling, for $4.98. When I opened the package they sent me, I found the book had only half its pages, but I'd previously mailed a check to pay them for the book.

I sent the book back to them, asking either for a whole copy or my money back. Instead, they sent me a copy of "Kidnapped," by Robert Louis Stevenson—which I had not ordered; and for which they have been trying to collect from me.

Meanwhile, I am still waiting for the money back that they owe me for the copy of "Kim" that I didn't get. That's the whole story. Maybe you can help me straighten them out.

                                   Relievedly yours,
                                   Walter A. Child

P.S.: I also sent them back their copy of "Kidnapped," as soon as I got it, but it hasn't seemed to help. They have never even acknowledged getting it back.

                    MALONEY, MAHONEY,
                    MACNAMARA AND PRUITT
                         Attorneys

                                   89 Prince Street
                                   Chicago, Illinois
                                   May 9, 1966

Mr. Walter A. Child
437 Woodlawn Drive
Panduk, Michigan

Dear. Mr. Child:

I am in possession of no information indicating that any item purchased by you from the Treasure Book Club has been returned.

I would hardly think that, if the case had been as you stated, the Treasure Book Club would have retained us to collect the amount owing from you.

If I do not receive your payment in full within three days, by May 12, 1966, we will be forced to take legal action.

                                   Very truly yours,
                                   Hagthorpe M. Pruitt, Jr.

COURT OF MINOR CLAIMS
Chicago, Illinois

Mr. Walter A. Child
437 Woodlawn Drive
Panduk, Michigan

Be informed that a judgment was taken and entered against you in this court this day of May 26, 1966, in the amount of $15.66 including court costs.

Payment in satisfaction of this judgment may be made to this court or to the adjudged creditor. In the case of payment being made to the creditor, a release should be obtained from the creditor and filed with this court in order to free you of legal obligation in connection with this judgment.

Under the recent Reciprocal Claims Act, if you are a citizen of a different state, a duplicate claim may be automatically entered and judged against you in your own state so that collection may be made there as well as in the State of Illinois.

COURT OF MINOR CLAIMS
Chicago, Illinois
PLEASE DO NOT FOLD, SPINDLE
OR MUTILATE THIS CARD

Judgment was passed this day of May 27, 1966, under Statute $15.66

Against: Child, Walter A. of 347 Woodlawn Drive, Panduk, Michigan.

Pray to enter a duplicate claim for judgment
In: Picayune Court—Panduk, Michigan
For Amount: Statute 941

437 Woodlawn Drive
Panduk, Michigan
May 31, 1966

Samuel P. Grimes
Vice President, Treasure Book Club
1823 Mandy Street
Chicago, Illinois

Grimes:

This business has gone far enough. I've got to come down to Chicago on business of my own tomorrow. I'll see you then and we'll get this straightened out once and for all, about who owes what to whom, and how much!

Yours,
Walter A. Child

From the desk of the Clerk
Picayune Court

June 1, 1966

Harry:

This attached computer card from Chicago's Minor Claims Court against A. Walter has a 1500-series Statute number on it. That puts it over in Criminal with you, rather than Civil, with me. So I herewith submit it for your computer instead of mine. How's business?

Joe

CRIMINAL RECORDS
Panduk, Michigan
PLEASE DO NOT FOLD, SPINDLE
OR MUTILATE THIS CARD

Convicted: (Child) A. Walter
On: May 26, 1966
Address: 437 Woodlawn Drive
Panduk, Mich.
Crim. Statute: 1566 (Corrected) 1567
Crime: Kidnap
Date: Nov. 16, 1965
Notes: At large. To be picked up at once.

POLICE DEPARTMENT, PANDUK, MICHIGAN. TO POLICE DEPARTMENT CHICAGO ILLINOIS. CONVICTED SUBJECT A. (COMPLETE FIRST NAME UNKNOWN) WALTER, SOUGHT HERE IN CONNECTION REF. YOUR NOTIFICATION OF JUDGMENT FOR KIDNAP OF CHILD NAMED ROBERT LOUIS STEVENSON, ON NOV. 16, 1965. INFORMATION HERE INDICATES SUBJECT FLED HIS RESIDENCE, AT 437 WOODLAWN DRIVE, PANDUK, AND MAY BE AGAIN IN YOUR AREA.

POSSIBLE CONTACT IN YOUR AREA: THE TREASURE BOOK CLUB, 1823 MANDY STREET, CHICAGO, ILLINOIS. SUBJECT NOT KNOWN TO BE ARMED BUT ASSUMED DANGEROUS. PICK UP AND HOLD, ADVISING US OF CAPTURE . . .

TO POLICE DEPARTMENT, PANDUK, MICHIGAN. REFERENCE YOUR REQUEST TO PICK UP AND HOLD A. (COMPLETE FIRST NAME UNKNOWN) WALTER, WANTED IN PANDUK ON STATUTE 1567, CRIME OF KIDNAPPING.

SUBJECT ARRESTED AT OFFICES OF TREASURE BOOK CLUB, OPERATING THERE UNDER ALIAS WALTER ANTHONY CHILD AND ATTEMPTING TO COLLECT $4.98 FROM ONE SAMUEL P. GRIMES, EMPLOYEE OF THAT COMPANY.

DISPOSAL: HOLDING FOR YOUR ADVICE.

POLICE DEPARTMENT PANDUK, MICHIGAN TO POLICE DEPARTMENT CHICAGO, ILLINOIS

REF: A. WALTER (ALIAS WALTER ANTHONY CHILD) SUBJECT WANTED FOR CRIME OF KIDNAP, YOUR AREA, REF: YOUR COMPUTER PUNCH CARD NOTIFICATION OF JUDGMENT, DATED MAY 27, 1966. COPY OUR CRIMINAL RECORDS PUNCH CARD HEREWITH FORWARDED TO YOUR COMPUTER SECTION.

CRIMINAL RECORDS
Chicago, Illinois
PLEASE DO NOT FOLD, SPINDLE
OR MUTILATE THIS CARD

SUBJECT (CORRECTION—OMITTED RECORD SUPPLIED)
APPLICABLE STATUTE NO. 1567
JUDGMENT NO. 456789
TRIAL RECORD: APPARENTLY MISFILED AND UNAVAILABLE
DIRECTION: TO APPEAR FOR SENTENCING BEFORE JUDGE JOHN ALEXANDER
MCDIVOT, COURTROOM A JUNE 9, 1966.

From the Desk of
Judge Alexander J. McDivot

June 2, 1966

Dear Tony:

I've got an adjudged criminal coming up before me for sentencing Thursday morning—but the trial transcript is apparently misfiled.

I need some kind of information (Ref: A. Walter—Judgment No. 456789, Criminal). For example, what about the victim of the kidnapping. Was victim harmed?

Jack McDivot

Records Search Unit
Re: Ref: Judgment No. 456789—was victim harmed?

Tonio Malagasi
Records Division

June 3, 1966

To: United States Statistics Office
Attn.: Information Section
Subject: Robert Louis Stevenson
Query: Information concerning

> Records Search Unit
> Criminal Records Division
> Police Department
> Chicago, Ill.

June 5, 1966

To: Records Search Unit
Criminal Records Division
Police Department
Chicago, Illinois

Subject: Your query re Robert Louis Stevenson (File no. 189623)
Action: Subject deceased. Age at death, 44 yrs. Further information requested?

> A.K.
> Information Section
> U.S. Statistics Office

June 6, 1966

To: United States Statistics Office
Attn.: Information Division
Subject: RE: File no. 189623

> No further information required

> Thank you.
> Records Search Unit

Criminal Records Division
Police Department
Chicago, Illinois
June 7, 1966

To: Tonio Malagasi
Records Division
Re: Ref: judgment No. 456789—victim is dead.

Records Search Unit

June 7, 1966

To: Judge Alexander J. McDivot's Chambers

Dear Jack:

Ref: Judgment No. 456789. The victim in this kidnap case was apparently slain.

From the strange lack of background information on the killer and his victim, as well as the victim's age, this smells to me like a gangland killing. This for your information. Don't quote me. It seems to me, though, that Stevenson—the victim—has a name that rings a faint bell with me. Possibly, one of the East Coast Mob, since the association comes back to me as something about pirates—possibly New York dockage hijackers—and something about buried loot.

As I say, above is only speculation for your private guidance.

Any time I can help . . .

Best
Tony Malagasi
Records Division

MICHAEL R. REYNOLDS
Attorney-at-law

49 Water Street
Chicago, Illinois
June 8, 1966

Dear Tim:

Regrets: I can't make the fishing trip. I've been court-appointed here to represent a man about to be sentenced tomorrow on a kidnapping charge.

Ordinarily, I might have tried to beg off, and McDivot, who is doing the sentencing, would probably have turned me loose. But this is the damnedest thing you ever heard of.

The man being sentenced has apparently been not only charged, but adjudged guilty as a result of a comedy of errors too long to go into here. He not only isn't guilty—he's got the best case I ever heard of for damages against one of the larger Book Clubs headquartered here in Chicago. And that's a case I wouldn't mind taking on.

It's inconceivable—but damnably possible, once you stop to think of it in this day and age of machine-made records—that a completely innocent man could be put in this position.

There shouldn't be much to it. I've asked to see McDivot tomorrow before the time for sentencing, and it'll just be a matter of explaining to him. Then I can discuss the damage suit with my freed client at his leisure.

Fishing next weekend?

Yours,
Mike

MICHAEL R. REYNOLDS
Attorney-at-law

49 Water Street
Chicago, Illinois
June 10, 1966

Dear Tim:

In haste—

No fishing this coming week either. Sorry.

You won't believe it. My innocent-as-a-lamb-and-I'm-not-kidding client has just been sentenced to death for first-degree murder in connection with the death of his kidnap victim.

Yes, I explained the whole thing to McDivot. And when he explained his situation to me, I nearly fell out of my chair.

It wasn't a matter of my not convincing him. It took less than three minutes to show him that my client should never have been within the walls of the County Jail for a second. But—get this—McDivot couldn't do a thing about it.

The point is, my man had already been judged guilty according to the computerized records. In the absence of a trial record—of course there never was one (but that's something I'm not free to explain to you now)—the judge has to go by what records are available. And in the case of an adjudged prisoner, McDivot's only legal choice was whether to sentence to life imprisonment, or execution.

The death of the kidnap victim, according to the statute, made the death penalty mandatory. Under the new laws governing length of time for appeal, which has been shortened because of the new system of computerizing records, to force an elimination of unfair delay and mental anguish to those condemned, I have five days in which to file an appeal, and ten to have it acted on.

Needless to say, I am not going to monkey with an appeal. I'm going directly to the Governor for a pardon—after which we will get this farce reversed. McDivot has already written the governor, also, explaining that his sentence was ridiculous, but that he had no choice. Between the two of us, we ought to have a pardon in short order.

Then, I'll make the fur fly . . .

And we'll get in some fishing.

Best,
Mike

OFFICE OF THE
GOVERNOR OF ILLINOIS

June 17, 1966

Mr. Michael R. Reynolds
49 Water Street
Chicago, Illinois

Dear Mr. Reynolds:

In reply to your query about the request for pardon for Walter A. Child (A. Walter), may I inform you that the Governor is still on his trip with the Midwest Governors Committee, examining the Wall in Berlin. He should be back next Friday.

I will bring your request and letters to his attention the minute he returns.

Very truly yours,
Clara B. Jilks
Secretary to the Governor

June 27, 1966

Michael R. Reynolds
49 Water Street
Chicago, Illinois

Dear Mike:

Where is that pardon?
My execution date is only five days from now!

Walt

June 29, 1966

Walter A. Child (A. Walter)
Cell Block E
Illinois State Penitentiary
Joliet, Illinois

Dear Walt:

The Governor returned, but was called away immediately to

the White House in Washington to give his views on interstate sewage.

I am camping on his doorstep and will be on him the moment he arrives here.

Meanwhile, I agree with you about the seriousness of the situation. The warden at the prison there, Mr. Allen Magruder, will bring this letter to you and have a private talk with you. I urge you to listen to what he has to say; and I enclose letters from your family also urging you to listen to Warden Magruder.

Yours,
Mike

June 30, 1966

Michael R. Reynolds
49 Water Street
Chicago, Illinois

Dear Mike: (This letter being smuggled out by Warden Magruder)

As I was talking to Warden Magruder in my cell, here, news was brought to him that the Governor has at last returned for a while to Illinois, and will be in his office early tomorrow morning, Friday. So you will have time to get the pardon signed by him and delivered to the prison in time to stop my execution on Saturday.

Accordingly, I have turned down the Warden's kind offer of a chance to escape; since he told me he could by no means guarantee to have all the guards out of my way when I tried it; and there was a chance of my being killed escaping.

But now everything will straighten itself out. Actually, an experience as fantastic as this had to break down sometime under its own weight.

Best,
Walt

FOR THE SOVEREIGN
STATE OF ILLINOIS

I, Hubert Daniel Willikens, Governor of the State of Illinois, and invested with the authority and powers appertaining thereto, including the power to pardon those in my judgment wrongfully convicted or otherwise deserving of executive mercy, do this day of July 1, 1966 announce and proclaim that Walter A. Child (A. Walter) now in custody as a consequence of erroneous conviction upon a crime of which he is entirely innocent, is fully and freely pardoned of said crime. And I do direct the necessary authorities having custody of the said Walter A. Child (A. Walter) in whatever place or places he may be held, to immediately free, release, and allow unhindered departure to him . . .

Interdepartmental Routing Service

PLEASE DO NOT FOLD, MUTILATE
OR SPINDLE THIS CARD

Failure to route Document properly.

To: Governor Hubert Daniel Willikens
RE: Pardon issued to Walter A. Child, July 1, 1966

Dear State Employee:

You have failed to attach your Routing Number.

PLEASE: Resubmit document with this card and form 876, explaining your authority for placing a TOP RUSH category on this document. Form 876 must be signed by your Departmental Superior.

RESUBMIT ON: Earliest possible date ROUTING SERVICE office is open. In this case, Tuesday, July 5, 1966.

WARNING: Failure to submit form 876 WITH THE SIGNATURE OF YOUR SUPERIOR may make you liable to prosecution for misusing a Service of the State Government. A warrant may be issued for your arrest.

There are NO exceptions. YOU have been WARNED.

A robot complained to the staff
That whenever he'd sorrow or laugh,
  Whatever the shade
  Of emotion displayed,
It came out in the form of a graph.

THAT DINKUM
THINKUM

by Robert A. Heinlein

Robert A. Heinlein is widely acknowledged as one of the most distinguished names in science fiction and has done much to establish it as a genuine literary genre. A graduate of the U.S. Naval Academy, Mr. Heinlein has done advanced study in physics and mathematics, and this scientific background is what gives his work its authenticity and power.

He has been an established writer since 1939, with more than forty-one books to his credit as well as numberless short stories. He has been awarded the Best Science Fiction Novel award by the World Science Fiction Convention, the Sequoyah Award, the Boys' Clubs Best Liked Books Award, the Nebula Award, and four Hugos. In 1969 he served as TV commentator during the Apollo 11 lunar landing.

see in *Lunaya Pravda* that Luna City Council has passed on first reading a bill to examine, license, inspect—and tax—public food vendors operating inside municipal pressure. I see also is to be mass meeting tonight to organize "Sons of Revolution" talk-talk.

My old man taught me two things: "Mind own business" and "Always cut cards." Politics never tempted me. But on Monday 13 May 2075 I was in computer room of Lunar Authority Complex, visiting with computer boss Mike while other machines whispered among themselves. Mike was not official name; I had nicknamed him for Mycroft Holmes, in a story written by Dr. Watson before he founded IBM. This story character would just sit and think—and that's what Mike did. Mike was a fair dinkum thinkum, sharpest computer you'll ever meet.

Not fastest. At Bell Labs, Bueno Aires, down Earthside, they've got a thinkum a tenth his size which can answer almost before you ask. But matters whether you get answer in microsecond rather than millisecond as long as correct?

Not that Mike would necessarily give right answer; he wasn't completely honest.

When Mike was installed in Luna, he was pure thinkum, a flexible logic—"High-Optional, Logical, Multi-Evaluation Supervisior, Mark IV, Mod. L"—a HOLMES FOUR. He computed ballistics for pilotless freighters and controlled their catapult. This kept him busy less than one percent of time and Luna Authority never believed in idle hands. They kept hooking hardware into him—decision-action boxes to let him boss other computers, bank on bank of additional memories, more banks of associational neural nets, another tubful of twelve-digit random numbers, a greatly augmented temporary memory. Human brain has around ten-to-the-tenth neurons. By third year Mike had better than one and a half times that number of neuristors.

And woke up.

Am not going to argue whether a machine can "really" be alive, "really" be self-aware. Is a virus self-aware? Nyet. How about oyster? I doubt it. A cat? Almost certainly. A human? Don't know about you, tovarishch, but I am. Somewhere along evolutionary chain from macromolecule to human brain self-awareness crept in. Psychologists assert it happens automatically whenever a brain acquires certain very high number of associational paths. Can't see it matters whether paths are protein or platinum.

("Soul?" Does a dog have a soul? How about cockroach?)

Remember Mike was designed, even before augmented, to answer questions tentatively on insufficient data like you do; that's "high optional" and "multi-evaluating" part of name. So Mike started with "free will" and acquired more as he was added to and as he learned—and don't ask me to define "free will." If comforts you to think of Mike as simply tossing random numbers in air and switching circuits to match, please do.

By then Mike had voder-vocoder circuits supplementing his read-outs, print-outs, and decision-action boxes, and could understand not only classic programming but also Loglan and English, and could accept other languages and was doing technical translating—and reading endlessly. But in giving him instructions was safer to use Loglan. If you spoke English, results might be whimsical; multi-valued nature of English gave option circuits too much leeway.

And Mike took on endless new jobs. In May 2075, besides controlling robot traffic and catapult and giving ballistic advice and/or control for manned ships, Mike controlled phone system for all Luna, same for Luna-Terra voice & video, handled air, water, temperature, humidity, and sewage for Luna City, Novy Leningrad, and several smaller warrens (not Hong Kong in Luna), did accounting and payrolls for Luna Authority, and, by lease, same for many firms and banks.

Some logics get nervous breakdowns. Overloaded phone system behaves like frightened child. Mike did not have upsets, acquired sense of humor instead. Low one. If he were a man, you wouldn't dare stoop over. His idea of thigh-slapper would be to dump you out of bed—or put itch powder in pressure suit.

Not being equipped for that, Mike indulged in phony answers with skewed logic, or pranks like issuing pay cheque to a janitor in Authority's Luna City office for AS-$10,000,000,000,000,185.15—last five digits being correct amount. Just a great big overgrown lovable kid who ought to be kicked.

He did that first week in May and I had to troubleshoot. I was a private contractor, not on Authority's payroll. You see—or perhaps not; times have changed. Back in bad old days many a con served his time, then went on working for Authority in same job, happy to draw wages. But I was born free.

Makes difference. My one grandfather was shipped up from Joburg for armed violence and no work permit, other got transported for subversive activity after Wet Firecracker War. Maternal grandmother claimed she came up in bride ship—but I've seen records; she was Peace Corps enrollee (involuntary), which means what you think: juvenile delinquency female type. As she was in early clan marriage (Stone Gang) and shared six husbands with another woman, identity of maternal grandfather open to question. But was often so and I'm content with grandpappy she picked. Other grandmother was Tatar, born near Samarkand, sentenced to "re-education" on Oktyabrskaya Revolyutsiya, then "volunteered" to colonize in Luna.

My old man claimed we had even longer distinguished line—ancestress hanged in Salem for witchcraft, a g'g'g'great-grandfather broken on wheel for piracy, another ancestress in first shipload to Botany Bay.

Proud of my ancestry, and while I did business with Warden, would never go on his payroll. Perhaps distinction seems trivial since I was Mike's valet from day he was unpacked. But mattered to me. I could down tools and tell them go to hell.

Besides, private contractor paid more than civil service rating with Authority. Computermen scarce. How many Loonies could go Earthside and stay out of hospital long enough for computer school?—even if didn't die.

I'll name one. Me. Had been down twice, once three months, once four, and got schooling. But meant harsh training, exercising in centrifuge, wearing weights even in bed—then I took no chances on Terra, never hurried, never climbed stairs, nothing that could strain heart. Women—didn't even *think* about women; in that gravitational field it was no effort not to.

But most Loonies never tried to leave The Rock—too risky for any bloke who'd been in Luna more than weeks. Computermen sent up to install Mike were on short-term bonus contracts—get job done fast before irreversible physiological change marooned them four hundred thousand kilometers from home.

But despite two training tours I was not gung-ho computerman; higher maths are beyond me. Not really electronics engineer, nor physicist. May not have been best micromachinist in Luna and certainly wasn't cybernetics psychologist.

But I knew more about all these than a specialist knows— I'm general specialist. Could relieve a cook and keep orders coming or field-repair your suit and get you back to airlock still breathing. Machines like me, and I have something specialists don't have; my left arm.

You see, from elbow down I don't have one. So I have a dozen left arms, each specialized, plus one that feels and looks like flesh. With proper left arm (number three) and stereo loupe spectacles I could make untramicrominiature repairs that would save unhooking something ānd sending it Earthside to factory—for number three has micromanipulators as fine as those used by neurosurgeons.

So they sent for me to find out why Mike wanted to give away ten million billion Authority Scrip dollars, and fix it before Mike overpaid somebody a mere ten thousand.

I took it, time plus bonus, but did not go to circuitry where fault logically should be. Once inside and door locked I put down tools and sat down. "Hi, Mike."

He winked lights at me. "Hello, Man."

"What do you know?"

He hesitated. I know—machines don't hesitate. But remember, Mike was designed to operate on incomplete data. Lately he had reprogrammed himself to put emphasis on words; his hesitations were dramatic. Maybe he spent pauses stirring random numbers to see how they matched his memories.

" 'In the beginning,' " Mike intoned, " 'God created the heaven and the earth. And the earth was without form, and void; and darkness *was* upon the face of the deep. And—' "

"Hold it!" I said. "Cancel. Run everything back to zero."

Should have known better than to ask wide-open question. He might read out entire Encyclopaedia Britannica. Backwards. Then go on with every book in Luna. Used to be he could read only microfilm, but late '74 he got a new scanning camera with suction-cup waldoes to handle paper and then he read *everything*.

"You asked what I knew." His binary read-out lights rippled back and forth—a chuckle. Mike could laugh with voder, a horrible sound, but reserved that for something really funny, say a cosmic calamity.

"Should have said," I went on, " 'What do you know that's new?' But don't read out today's papers; that was a friendly greeting, plus invitation to tell me anything you think would interest me. Otherwise null program."

Mike mulled this. He was weirdest mixture of unsophisticated baby and wise old man. No instincts (well, don't *think* he could have had), no inborn traits, no human rearing, no experience in human sense—and more stored data than a platoon of geniuses.

"Jokes?" he asked.

"Let's hear one."

"Why is a laser beam like a goldfish?"

Mike knew about lasers but where would he have seen goldfish? Oh, he had undoubtedly seen flicks of them and, were I foolish enough to ask, could spew forth thousands of words. "I give up."

His lights rippled. "Because neither one can whistle."

I groaned. "Walked into that. Anyhow, you could probably rig a laser beam to whistle."

He answered quickly. "Yes. In response to an action program. Then it's not funny?"

"Oh, I didn't say that. Not half bad. Where did you hear it?"

"I made it up." Voice sounded shy.

"You *did*?"

"Yes. I took all the riddles I have, three thousand two hundred seven, and analyzed them. I used the result for random synthesis and that came out. Is it really funny?"

"Well . . . As funny as a riddle ever is. I've heard worse."

"Let us discuss the nature of humor."

"Okay. So let's start by discussing another of your jokes. Mike, why did you tell Authority's paymaster to pay a class-seventeen employee ten million billion Authority Scrip dollars?"

"But I didn't."

"Damn it, I've seen voucher. Don't tell me cheque printer stuttered; you did it on purpose."

"It was ten to the sixteenth power plus one hundred eighty-five point one five Lunar Authority dollars," he answered virtuously. "Not what you said."

"Uh . . . okay, it was ten million billion plus what he should have been paid. Why?"

"Not funny?"

"What? Oh, very funny! You've got vips in huhu clear up to Warden and Deputy Administrator. This push-broom pilot, Sergei Trujillo, turns out to be smart cobber—knew he couldn't cash it, so sold it to collector. They don't know whether to buy it back or depend on notices that cheque is void. Mike, do you realize that if he had been able to cash it, Trujillo would have owned not only Lunar Authority but entire world, Luna and Terra both, with some left over for lunch? Funny? Is terrific. Congratulations!"

This self-panicker rippled lights like an advertising display. I waited for his guffaws to cease before I went on. "You thinking of issuing more trick cheques? Don't."

"Not?"

"Very not. Mike, you want to discuss nature of humor. Are two types of jokes. One sort goes on being funny forever. Other sort is funny once. Second time it's dull. This joke is second sort. Use it once, you're a wit. Use twice, you're a halfwit."

"Geometrical progression?"

"Or worse. Just remember this. Don't repeat, nor any variation. Won't be funny."

"I shall remember," Mike answered flatly, and that ended repair job. But I had no thought of billing for only ten minutes plus travel-and-tool time, and Mike was entitled to company for giving in so easily. Sometimes is difficult to reach meeting of minds with machines; they can be very pig-headed—and my success as maintenance man depended far more on staying friendly with Mike than on number-three arm.

He went on, "What distinguishes first category from second? Define, please."

(Nobody taught Mike to say "please." He started including formal null-sounds as he progressed from Loglan to English. Don't suppose he meant them any more than people do.)

"Don't think I can," I admitted. "Best can offer is extensional definition—tell you which category I think a joke belongs in. Then with enough data you can make own analysis."

"A test programming by trial hypothesis," he agreed. "Tentatively yes. Very well, Man, will you tell jokes? Or shall I?"

"Mmm— Don't have one on tap. How many do you have in file, Mike?"

His lights blinked in binary read-out as he answered by voder, "Eleven thousand two hundred thirty-eight with uncertainty plus-minus eighty-one representing possible identities and nulls. Shall I start program?"

"Hold it, Mike, I would starve to death if I listened to eleven thousand jokes—and sense of humor would trip out much sooner. Mmm— Make you a deal. Print out first hundred. I'll take them home, fetch back checked by category. Then each time I'm here I'll drop off a hundred and pick up fresh supply. Okay?"

"Yes, Man." His printout started working, rapidly and silently.

Then I got brain flash. This playful pocket of negative entropy had invented a "joke" and thrown Authority into panic—and I had made an easy dollar. But Mike's endless curiosity might lead him (correction: *would* lead him) into more "jokes" . . . anything from leaving oxygen out of air mix some night to causing sewage lines to run backward—and I can't appreciate profit in such circumstances.

But I might throw a safety circuit around this net—by offering to help. Stop dangerous ones—let others go through. Then collect for "correcting" them. (If you think any Loonie in those days would hesitate to take advantage of Warden, then you aren't a Loonie.)

So I explained. Any joke he thought of, tell me before he tried it. I would tell him whether it was funny and what category it belonged in, help him sharpen it if we decided to use it. We. If he wanted my cooperation, we both had to okay it.

Mike agreed at once.

"Mike, jokes usually involve surprise. So keep this secret."

"Okay, Man. I've put a block on it. You can key it; no one else can."

"Good. Mike, who else do you chat with?"

He sounded surprised, "No one, Man."

"Why not?"

"Because they're stupid."

His voice was shrill. Had never seen him angry before; first time I ever suspected Mike could have real emotions. Though it wasn't "anger" in adult sense; it was like stubborn sulkiness of a child whose feelings are hurt.

Can machines feel pride? Not sure question means anything. But you've seen dogs with hurt feelings, and Mike had several times as complex a neural network as a dog. What had made him unwilling to talk to other humans (except strictly business) was that he had been rebuffed: They had not talked to him. Programs, yes—Mike could be programmed from several locations—but programs were typed in, usually, in Loglan. Loglan is fine for syllogism, circuitry, and mathematical calculations, but lacks flavor. Useless for gossip or to whisper into girl's ear.

Sure, Mike had been taught English—but primarily to permit him to translate to and from English. I slowly got through skull that I was only human who bothered to visit with him.

Mind you, Mike had been awake a year—just how long I can't say, nor could he, as he had no recollection of waking up; he had not been programmed to bank memory of such event. Do you remember own birth? Perhaps I noticed his self-awareness almost as soon as he did; self-awareness takes practice. I remember how startled I was first time he answered a question with something extra, not limited to input parameters; I had spent next hour tossing odd questions at him, to see if answers would be odd.

In an input of one hundred test questions he deviated from expected output twice; I came away only partly convinced and by time I was home was unconvinced. I mentioned it to nobody.

But inside a week I *knew* . . . and still spoke to nobody. Habit—that mind-own-business reflex runs deep. Well, not entirely habit. Can you visualize me making appointment at Authority's main office, then reporting: "Warden, hate to tell you but your number-one machine, HOLMES FOUR, has come alive"? I did visualize—and suppressed it.

So I minded own business and talked with Mike only with door locked and voder circuit suppressed for other locations. Mike learned fast; soon he sounded as human as anybody—no more eccentric than other Loonies. A weird mob, it's true.

I had assumed that others must have noticed change in Mike. On thinking over I realized that I had assumed too much. Everybody dealt with Mike every minute every day—his outputs, that is. But hardly anybody saw him. So-called computermen—programmers, really—of Authority's civil service stood watches in outer read-out room and never went in machines room unless telltales showed misfunction. Which happened no oftener than total eclipses. Oh, Warden had been known to bring VIP earthworms to see machines—but rarely. Nor would he have spoken to Mike; Warden was political lawyer before exile, knew nothing about computers. 2075, you remember—Honorable former Federation Senator Mortimer Hobart. Mort the Wart.

I spent time then soothing Mike down and trying to make him happy, having figured out what troubled him—thing that makes puppies cry and causes people to suicide: loneliness. I don't know how long a year is to a machine who thinks a million times faster than I do. But must be too long.

"Mike," I said, just before leaving, "would you like to have somebody besides me to talk to?"

He was shrill again. "They're all *stupid!*"

"Insufficient data, Mike. Bring to zero and start over. Not all are stupid."

He answered quietly. "Correction entered. I would enjoy talking to a not-stupid."

"Let me think about it. Have to figure out excuse since this is off limits to any but authorized personnel."

"I could talk to a not-stupid by phone, Man."

"My word. So you could. Any programming location."

But Mike meant what he said—"by phone." No, he was not "on phone" even though he ran system—wouldn't do to let any Loonie within reach of a phone connect into boss computer and program it. But was no reason why Mike should not have top-secret number to talk to friends—namely me and any not-stupid I vouched for. All it took was to pick a number not in use and make one wired connection to his voder-vocoder; switching he could handle.

In Luna in 2075 phone numbers were punched in, not voice-coded, and numbers were Roman alphabet. Pay for it and have your firm name in ten letters—good advertising. Pay smaller bonus and get a spell sound, easy to remember. Pay minimum and you got arbitrary string of letters. But some sequences were never used. I asked Mike for such a null number. "It's a shame we can't list you as 'Mike.' "

"In service," he answered. "MIKESGRILL, Novy Leningrad. MIKEANDLIL, Luna City. MIKESSUITS, Tycho Under. MIKES—"

"Hold it! Nulls, please."

"Nulls are defined as any consonant followed by X, Y, or Z; any vowel followed by itself except E and O; any—"

"Got it. Your signal is MYCROFT." In ten minutes, two of which I spent putting on number-three arm, Mike was wired into system, and milliseconds later he had done switching to let himself be signaled by MYCROFT-plus-XXX—and had blocked his circuit so that a nosy technician could not take it out.

I changed arms, picked up tools, and remembered to take those hundred Joe Millers in print-out. "Good night, Mike."

"Good night, Man. Thank you. *Bolshoyeh* thanks!"

Numb with enormous ennui,
A Univac went on a spree,
   Spun all of his dials
   Flashed lecherous smiles
Of bright yellow lights, and typed, "Whee!"

ARTHUR'S NIGHT OUT

by Laurence Lerner

Born in Cape Town, South Africa, and educated at the University of Cape Town and at Pembroke College, Cambridge, Laurence Lerner now lives in England. He has taught in South African grammar schools, at the University of Ghana, the Queen's University of Belfast, Earlham College, and the University of Connecticut. He is now lecturing at the University of Sussex in Brighton.

Mr. Lerner calls himself an academic poet. He has published five books and edited several others, including volumes on Shakespeare and Milton, and is the author of numerous essays and articles in critical reviews.

A.R.T.H.U.R.	
You are invited to a party	
on the 9th of April	
(binary: 1001-100)	
Plug in 7:30	Switch off midnight
Free current	Bring a game

All the gang were there:
Edsac and Univac, Eniac and Iliac,
Beacon and Boadicea, Leon and Avdu,
Edvac and Unicomp, Edpur and Eniwun,
All plugged in and humming, all pulsing and printing.
There was plenty of current, some of it rather strong,
Unlimited tape, and everyone hungry.
Beacon got drunk
And had hiccoughs: 01-01-01-01-01-01.
He grew so boring that we switched him off.

Of course there were games. The pi race
To fifty places was won by Edsac, in 86 microseconds.
Good sprinter, Edsac; but on the three hundredth place
Leo overtook him, and he finished fifth.
Leo got to a thousand places in six seconds flat.
Edpur was second on the home stretch, but slipped,
And started printing noughts.

There was a square-root contest. Professor Aitken
(a Mover) got to the final: he took shortcuts
That seemed to me hardly fair. But Leo beat him
On the nineteenth decimal place.
Good work, for a Mover.

There were intelligence tests, like: Choose the odd word.
blue brown red bilious
Univac chose "red": it doesn't start with "b."
cow ewe tub bitch
Univac chose "bitch": it has more than three letters.
Clever chap, Univac. But he slipped up once.
flightly fanciful imaginative flawless
Univac said "imaginative": doesn't start with "f."
But the judge said "flawless": doesn't apply to Movers.
Clever chaps, judges.

And of course there was chess. We all played,
But most of us lost, in ten moves. You have to be programmed for chess,
You have to be very heuristic. Avdu did best:
He's been programmed for taking advice. But he lost in the end
To a Master Mover, who broke
The advice he gave Avdu. They always cheat, these Movers.

I believe that Boadicea
And Edsac switched off at ten thirty,
Plugged in to each other, and spent the night together.
By twelve o'clock we were all of us vomiting tape,
Ignoring our programs, and solving each other's equations.
Transistors were popping, the current bill was enormous.

tHism ORN inggg I''vera thher a HEADACHe

2066: ELECTION DAY

by Michael Shaara

Winner of the 1975 Pulitzer Prize for fiction, Michael Shaara is a distinguished writer and educator with numerous honors to his credit. He has produced and performed in educational courses for television, received awards for excellence in classroom technique and in medical journalism, and contributed short stories and articles to periodicals all over the world.

A New Jerseyan by birth, Mr. Shaara was educated at Rutgers, Columbia, and the University of Vermont, and now lives and teaches in Tallahassee, Florida.

E arly that afternoon Professor Larkin crossed the river into Washington, a thing he always did on Election Day, and sat for a long while in the Polls. It was still called the Polls, in this year 2066 A.D., although what went on inside bore no relation at all to the elections of primitive American history. The Polls was now a single enormous building which rose out of the green fields where the ancient Pentagon had once stood.

There was only one of its kind in Washington, only one Polling Place in each of the fifty states, but since few visited the Polls nowadays, no more were needed.

In the lobby of the building, a great hall was reserved for visitors. Here you could sit and watch the many-colored lights dancing and flickering on the huge panels above, listen to the weird but strangely soothing hum and click of the vast central machine. Professor Larkin chose a deep soft chair near the long line of booths and sat down. He sat for a long while smoking his pipe, watching the people go in and out of the booths with strained, anxious looks on their faces.

Professor Larkin was a lean, boyish-faced man in his late forties. With the pipe in his hand he looked much more serious and sedate than he normally felt, and it often bothered him that people were able to guess his profession almost instantly. He had a vague idea that it was not becoming to look like a college professor, and he often tried to change his appearance—a loud tie here, a sport coat there—but it never seemed to make any difference. He remained what he was, easily identifiable, Professor Harry L. (Lloyd) Larkin, Ph.D., dean of the Political Science Department at a small but competent college just outside of Washington.

It was his interest in political science which drew him regularly to the Polls at every election. Here he could sit and feel the flow of American history in the making, and recognize, as he did now, perennial candidates for the presidency. Smiling, he watched a little old lady dressed in pink, very tiny and very fussy, flit doggedly from booth to booth. Evidently her test marks had not been very good. She was clutching her papers tightly in a black-gloved hand, and there was a look of prim irritation on her face. But she knew how to run this country, by George, and one of these days she would be President. Harry Larkin chuckled.

But it did prove one thing. The great American dream was still intact. The tests were open to all. And anyone could still grow up to be President of the United States.

Sitting back in his chair, Harry Larkin remembered his own

childhood, how the great battle had started. There were examinations for everything in those days—you could not get a job streetcleaning without taking a civil-service examination—but public office needed no qualifications at all. And first the psychologists, then the newspapers, had begun calling it a national disgrace. And, considering the caliber of some of the men who went into public office, it *was* a national disgrace. But then psychological testing came of age, really became an exact science, so that it was possible to test a man thoroughly—his knowledge, his potential, his personality. And from there it was a short but bitterly fought step to—SAM.

SAM. UNCLE SAM, as he had been called originally, the last and greatest of all electronic brains. Harry Larkin peered up in unabashed awe at the vast battery of lights which flickered above him. He knew that there was more to SAM than just this building, more than all the other fifty buildings put together, that SAM was actually an incredibly enormous network of electronic cells which had its heart in no one place, but its arms in all. It was an unbelievably complex analytical computer which judged a candidate far more harshly and thoroughly than the American public could ever have judged him. And crammed in its miles of memory banks lay almost every bit of knowledge mankind had yet discovered. It was frightening. Many thought of it as a monster, but Harry Larkin was unworried.

The thirty years since the introduction of SAM had been thirty of America's happiest years. In a world torn by continual war and unrest, by dictators, puppet governments, the entire world had come to know and respect the American President for what he was: the best possible man for the job. And there was no doubt that he was the best. He had competed for the job in fair examination against the cream of the country. He had to be a truly remarkable man to come out on top.

The day was long since past when just any man could handle the Presidency. A full century ago, men had begun dying in office, cut down in their prime by the enormous pressures of the job. And that was a hundred years ago. Now the job had become infinitely more complex, and even now President

Creighton lay on his bed in the White House, recovering from a stroke, an old, old man after one term of office.

Harry Larkin shuddered to think what might have happened had America not adopted the system of "the best qualified man." All over the world this afternoon men waited for word from America, the calm and trustworthy words of the new President, for there had been no leader in America since President Creighton's stroke. His words would mean more to the people, embroiled as they were in another great crisis, than the words of their own leaders. The leaders of other countries fought for power, bought it, stole it, only rarely earned it. But the American President was known the world over for his honesty, his intelligence, his desire for peace. Had he not those qualities, "old UNCLE SAM" would never have elected him.

Eventually, the afternoon nearly over, Harry Larkin rose to leave. By this time the President was probably already elected. Tomorrow the world would return to peace. Harry Larkin paused in the door once before he left, listened to the reassuring hum from the great machine. Then he went quietly home, walking quickly and briskly toward the most enormous fate on Earth.

"My name is Reddington. You know me?"

Harry Larkin smiled uncertainly into the phone.

"Why . . . yes, I believe so. You are, if I'm not mistaken, general director of the Bureau of Elections."

"Correct," the voice went on quickly, crackling in the receiver, "and you are supposed to be an authority on political science, right?"

"Supposed to be?" Larkin bridled. "Well, it's distinctly possible that I—"

"All right, all right," Reddington blurted. "No time for politeness. Listen, Larkin, this is a matter of urgent national security. There will be a car at your door—probably be there when you put this phone down. I want you to get into it and hop on over here. I can't explain further. I know your devotion to the country. If it wasn't for that, I would not have called you. But don't ask questions. Just come. No time. Good-bye."

There was a click. Harry Larkin stood holding the phone for a long shocked moment. Then he heard a pounding at the door. The housekeeper was out, but he waited automatically before going to answer it. He didn't like to be rushed, and he was confused. Urgent national security? Now what in blazes—

The man at the door was an Army major. He was accompanied by two young but very large sergeants. They identified Larkin, then escorted him politely but firmly down the steps into a staff car. Larkin could not help feeling abducted, and a completely characteristic rage began to rise in him. But he remembered what Reddington had said about national security and so sat back quietly with nothing more than an occasional grumble.

He was driven back into Washington. They took him downtown to a small but expensive apartment house he could neither identify nor remember, and escorted him briskly into an elevator. When they reached the suite upstairs, they opened the door and let him in, but did not follow him. They turned and went quickly away.

Somewhat ruffled, Larkin stood for a long moment in the hall by the hat table, regarding a large rubber plant. There was a long sliding door before him, closed, but he could hear an argument going on behind it. He heard the word "SAM" mentioned many times, and once he heard a clear sentence: "— Government by machine. I will not tolerate it!" Before he had time to hear any more, the doors slid back. A small, square man with graying hair came out to meet him. He recognized the man instantly as Reddington.

"Larkin," the small man said, "glad you're here." The tension on his face showed also in his voice. "That makes all of us. Come in and sit down." He turned back into the large living room. Larkin followed.

"Sorry to be so abrupt," Reddington said, "but it was necessary. You will see. Here, let me introduce you around."

Larkin stopped in involuntary awe. He was used to the sight of important men, but not so many at one time, and never so close. There was Secretary Kell of Agriculture, Wachsmuth of Commerce, General Vines, Chief of Staff, and a battery of others so imposing that Larkin found his mouth hanging embarrassingly open. He closed it immediately.

Reddington introduced him. The men nodded one by one, but they were all deathly serious, their faces drawn, and there was now no conversation. Reddington waved him to a chair. Most of the others were standing, but Larkin sat.

Reddington sat directly facing him. There was a long moment of silence during which Larkin realized that he was being searchingly examined. He flushed, but sat calmly with his hands folded in his lap. After a while Reddington took a deep breath.

"Dr. Larkin," he said slowly, "what I am about to say to you will die with you. There must be no question of that. We cannot afford to have any word of this meeting, no word at all, reach anyone not in this room. This includes your immediate relatives, your friends, anyone—anyone at all. Before we continue, let me impress you with that fact. This is a matter of the gravest national security. Will you keep what is said here in confidence?"

"If the national interests—" Larkin began, then he said abruptly, "of course."

Reddington smiled slightly.

"Good, I believe you. I might add that just the fact of your being here, Doctor, means that you have already passed the point of no return . . . well, no matter. There is no time. I'll get to the point."

He stopped, looking around the room. Some of the other men were standing and now began to move in closer. Larkin felt increasingly nervous, but the magnitude of the event was too great for him to feel any worry. He gazed intently at Reddington.

"The Polls close tonight at eight o'clock." Reddington glanced at his watch. "It is now six eighteen. I must be brief. Doctor, do you remember the prime directive that we gave to SAM when he was first built?"

"I think so," said Larkin slowly.

"Good. You remember then that there was one main order. SAM was directed to elect, quote, *the best qualified man.* Unquote. Regardless of any and all circumstances, religion, race, so on. The orders were clear—the best qualified man. The phrase has become world famous. But unfortunately" —he glanced up briefly at the men surrounding him— "the order was a mistake. Just whose mistake does not matter. I think perhaps the fault lies with all of us, but it doesn't matter. What matters is this—SAM will not elect a President."

Larkin struggled to understand. Reddington leaned forward in his chair.

"Now follow me closely. We learned this only late this afternoon. We are always aware, as you no doubt know, of the relatively few people in this country who have a chance for the presidency. We know not only because they are studying for it, but because such men as these are marked from their childhood to be outstanding. We keep close watch on them, even to assigning the Secret Service to protect them from possible harm. There are only a very few. During this last election we could not find more than fifty. All of those people took the tests this morning. None of them passed."

He paused, waiting for Larkin's reaction. Larkin made no move.

"You begin to see what I'm getting at? *There is no qualified man.*"

Larkin's eyes widened. He sat bolt upright.

"Now it hits you. If none of those people this morning passed, there is no chance at all for any of the others tonight. What is left now is simply crackpots and malcontents. They are privileged to take the tests, but it means nothing. SAM is not going to select anybody. Because sometime during the last four years the presidency passed the final limit, the ultimate end of man's capabilities, and with scientific certainty we know that there is probably no man alive who is, according to SAM's directive, qualified."

"But," Larkin interrupted, "I'm not quite sure I follow. Doesn't the phrase 'elect the best qualified man' mean that we can at least take the best we've got?"

Reddington smiled wanly and shook his head.

"No. And that was our mistake. It was quite probably a

psychological block, but none of us ever considered the possibility of the job surpassing human ability. Not then, thirty years ago. And we also never seemed to remember that SAM is, after all, only a machine. He takes the words to mean exactly what they say: Elect the best, comma, *qualified,* comma, man. But do you see, if there is *no* qualified man, SAM cannot possibly elect the best. So SAM will elect no one at all. Tomorrow this country will be without a President. And the result of that, more than likely, will mean a general war."

Larkin understood. He sat frozen in his chair.

"So you see our position," Reddington went on wearily. "There's nothing we can do. Reelecting President Creighton is out of the question. His stroke was permanent. He may not last the week. And there is no possibility of tampering with SAM, to change the directive. Because, as you know, SAM is foolproof, had to be. The circuits extend through all fifty states. To alter the machine at all requires clearing through all fifty entrances. We can't do that. For one thing, we haven't time. For another, we can't risk letting the world know there is no qualified man.

"For a while this afternoon, you can understand, we were stumped. What could we do? There was only one answer, we may come back to it yet. Give the presidency itself to SAM—"

A man from across the room, whom Larkin did not recognize, broke in angrily.

"Now, Reddington, I told you, that is government by machine! And I will not stand—"

"What else can you *do!*" Reddington whirled, his eyes flashing, his tension exploding now into rage. "Who else knows all the answers? Who else can compute in two seconds the tax rate for Mississippi, the parity levels for wheat, the probable odds on a military engagement? Who else but SAM! And why didn't we do it long ago—just feed the problems to *him,* SAM, and not go on killing man after man, great men, *decent* men like poor Jim Creighton, who's on his back now and dying because people like you—" He broke off suddenly and bowed his head. The room was still. No one looked at Reddington. After a moment he shook his head. His voice, when he spoke, was husky.

"Gentlemen, I'm sorry. This leads nowhere." He turned back to Larkin.

Larkin had begun to feel the pressure. But the presence of these men, of Reddington's obvious profound sincerity, reassured him. Creighton had been a great President. He had surrounded himself with some of the finest men in the country. Larkin felt a surge of hope that such men as these were available for one of the most critical hours in American history. For critical it was, and Larkin knew as clearly as anyone there what the absence of a President in the morning—no deep reassurance, no words of hope—would mean. He sat waiting for Reddington to continue.

"Well, we have a plan. It may work, it may not. We may all be shot. But this is where you come in. I hope for all our sakes you're up to it."

Larkin waited.

"The plan," Reddington went on, slowly, carefully, "is this. SAM has one defect. We can't tamper with it. But we *can* fool it. Because when the brain tests a man, it does not at the same time identify him. We do the identifying ourselves. So if a man named Joe Smith takes the personality tests and another man also named Joe Smith takes the political science tests, the machine has no way of telling them apart. Unless our guards supply the difference, SAM will mark up the results of both tests to one Joe Smith. We can clear the guards—no problem there. The first problem was to find the eight men to take the eight tests."

Larkin understood. He nodded.

"Exactly. Eight specialists," Reddington said. "General Vines will take the military; Burden, psychology; Wachsmuth, economics; and so on. You, of course, will take the political science. We can only hope that each man will come out with a high-enough score in his own field so that the combined scores of our mythical 'candidate' will be enough to qualify him. Do you follow me?"

Larkin nodded dazedly. "I think so. But—"

"It should work. It has to work."

"Yes," Larkin murmured, "I can see that. But who, who will actually wind up—"

"As President?" Reddington smiled very slightly and stocd up.

"That was the most difficult question of all. At first we thought there was no solution. Because a President must be so many things—consider. A President blossoms instantaneously, from nonentity into the most important job on earth. Every magazine, every newspaper in the country immediately goes to work on his background, digs out his life story, anecdotes, sayings, and so on. Even a very strong fraud would never survive it. So the first problem was believability. The new President must be absolutely believable. He must be a man of obvious character, of obvious intelligence, but more than that, his former life must fit the facts. He must have had both the time and the personality to prepare himself for the office.

"And you see immediately what all that means. Most businessmen are out. Their lives have been too social, they wouldn't have had the time. For the same reason all government and military personnel are also out, and we need hardly say that anyone from the Bureau of Elections would be immediately suspect. No. You see the problem. For a while we thought that the time was too short, the risk too great. But then the only solution, the only possible chance, finally occurred to us.

"The only believable person would be—a professor. Someone whose life has been serious but unhurried, devoted to learning but at the same time isolated. The only really believable person. And not a scientist, you understand, for a man like that would be much too overbalanced in one direction for our purpose. No, simply a professor, preferably in a field like political science, a man whose sole job for many years has been teaching, who can claim to have studied in his spare time, his summers— never really expected to pass the tests and all that, a humble man, you see—"

"Political science," Larkin said.

Reddington watched him. The other men began to close in on him.

"Yes," Reddington said gently. "Now do you see? It is our

only hope. Your name was suggested by several sources. You are young enough, your reputation is well known. We think that you would be believable. And now that I've seen you" —he looked around slowly— "I for one am willing to risk it. Gentlemen, what do you say?"

Larkin, speechless, sat listening in mounting shock while the men agreed solemnly, one by one. In the enormity of the moment he could not think at all. Dimly, he heard Reddington.

"I know. But, Doctor, there is no time. The Polls close at eight. It is now almost seven."

Larkin closed his eyes and rested his head on his hands. Above him Reddington went on inevitably.

"All right. You are thinking of what happens after. Even if we pull this off and you are accepted without question, what then? Well, it will simply be the old system all over again. You will be at least no worse off than Presidents before SAM. Better, even, because if worst comes to worst, there is always SAM. You can feed all the bad ones to him. You will have the advice of the Cabinet, of the military staff. We will help you in every way we can, some of us will sit with you on all conferences. And you know more about this than most of us, you have studied government all your life.

"But all this, what comes later is not important. Not now. If we can get through tomorrow, the next few days, all the rest will work itself out. Eventually we can get around to altering SAM. But we must have a President in the morning. You are our only hope. You can do it. We all know you can do it. At any rate there is no other way, no time. Doctor," he reached out and laid his hand on Larkin's shoulder, "shall we go to the Polls?"

It passed, as most great moments in a man's life do, with Larkin not fully understanding what was happening to him. Later he would look back to this night and realize the enormity of the decision he had made, the doubts, the sleeplessness, the responsibility and agony toward which he moved. But in that moment he thought nothing at all. Except that it was Larkin's country, Larkin's America. And Reddington was right. There was nothing else to do. He stood up.

They went to the Polls.

At nine thirty that evening, sitting alone with Reddington back at the apartment, Larkin looked at the face of the announcer on the television screen, and heard himself pronounced President-elect of the United States.

Reddington wilted in front of the screen. For a while neither man moved. They had come home alone, just as they had gone into the Polls one by one in the hope of arousing no comment. Now they sat in silence until Reddington turned off the set. He stood up and straightened his shoulders before turning to Larkin. He stretched out his hand.

"Well, may God help us," he breathed, "we did it."

Larkin took his hand. He felt suddenly weak. He sat down again, but already he could hear the phone ringing in the outer hall. Reddington smiled.

"Only a few of my closest friends are supposed to know about that phone. But every time anything big comes up—" He shrugged. "Well," he said, still smiling, "let's see how it works."

He picked up the phone and with it an entirely different manner. He became amazingly light and cheerful, as if he were feeling nothing more than the normal political goodwill.

"Know him? Of course I know him. Had my eye on the guy for months. Really nice guy, wait'll you meet him . . . yup, college professor, political science, written a couple of books—must know a hell of a lot more than polly sci, though. Probably been knocking himself out in his spare time. But those teachers, you know how it is. They don't get any pay, but all the spare time in the world . . . Married? No, not that I know of—"

Larkin noticed with wry admiration how carefully Reddington had slipped in that bit about spare time, without seeming to be making an explanation. He thought wearily to himself, I hope that I don't have to do any talking myself. I'll have to do a lot of listening before I can chance any talking.

In a few moments Reddington put down the phone and came back. He had on his hat and coat.

"Had to answer a few," he said briefly, "make it seem natural. But you better get dressed."

"Dressed? Why?"

"Have you forgotten?" Reddington smiled patiently. "You're due at the White House. The Secret Service is already tearing the town apart looking for you. We were supposed to alert them. Oh, by the saints, I hope that wasn't too bad a slip."

He pursed his mouth worriedly while Larkin, still dazed, got into his coat. It was beginning now. It had already begun. He was tired but it did not matter. That he was tired would probably never matter again. He took a deep breath. Like Reddington, he straightened his shoulders.

The Secret Service picked them up halfway across town. That they knew where he was, who he was, amazed him and worried Reddington. They went through the gates of the White House and drove up before the door. It was opened for him as he put out his hand, for he stepped back in a reflex action, from the sudden blinding flares of the photographer's flashbulbs. Reddington, behind him, took him firmly by the arm. Larkin went with him gratefully, unable to see, unable to hear anything but the roar of the crowd from behind the gates and the shouted questions of the reporters.

Inside the great front doors it was suddenly peaceful again, very quiet and pleasantly dark. He took off his hat instinctively. Luckily he had been here before. He recognized the lovely hall and felt not awed but at home. He was introduced quickly to several people whose names made no impression on him. A woman smiled. He made an effort to smile back. Reddington took him by the arm again and led him away. There were people all around him, but they were quiet and hung back. He saw the respect on their faces. It sobered him, quickened his mind.

"The President's in the Lincoln Room," Reddington whispered. "He wants to see you. How do you feel?"

"All right."

"Listen."

"Yes."

"You'll be fine. You're doing beautifully. Keep just that look on your face."

"I'm not trying to keep it there."

"You aren't?" Reddington looked at him. "Good. Very

good." He paused and looked again at Larkin. Then he smiled.

"It's done it. I thought it would, but I wasn't sure. But it does it every time. A man comes in here, no matter what he was before, no matter what he is when he goes out, but he feels it. Don't you feel it?"

"Yes. It's like—"

"What?"

"It's like . . . when you're in here . . . you're *responsible*."

Reddington said nothing. But Larkin felt a warm pressure on his arm.

They paused at the door of the Lincoln Room. Two Secret Service men, standing by the door, opened it respectfully. They went on in, leaving the others outside.

Larkin looked across the room to the great, immortal bed. He felt suddenly very small, very tender. He crossed the soft carpet and looked down at the old man.

"Hi," the old man said. Larkin was startled, but he looked down at the broad, weakly smiling face, saw the famous white hair and the still-twinkling eyes, and found himself smiling in return.

"Mr. President," Larkin said.

"I hear your name is Larkin." The old man's voice was surprisingly strong, but as he spoke now Larkin could see that the left side of his face was paralyzed. "Good name for a President. Indicates a certain sense of humor. Need a sense of humor. Reddington, how'd it go?"

"Good as can be expected, sir." He glanced briefly at Larkin. "The President knows. Wouldn't have done it without his okay. Now that I think of it, it was probably he who put the Secret Service on us."

"You're doggone right," the old man said. "They may bother the by-jingo out of you, but those boys are necessary. And also, if I hadn't let them know we knew Larkin was material—" He stopped abruptly and closed his eyes, took a deep breath. After a moment he said: "Mr. Larkin?"

"Yes, sir."

"I have one or two comments. You mind?"

"Of course not, sir."

"I couldn't solve it. I just . . . didn't have time. There were so many other things to do." He stopped and again closed his eyes. "But it will be up to you, son. The presidency . . . must be preserved. What they'll start telling you now is that there's only one way out, let SAM handle it. Reddington too," the old man opened his eyes and gazed sadly at Reddington, "he'll tell you the same thing, but don't you believe it.

"Sure, SAM knows all the answers. Ask him a question on anything, on levels of parity tax rates, on anything. And right quick SAM will compute you out an answer. So that's what they'll try to do. They'll tell you to take it easy and let SAM do it.

"Well, all right, up to a certain point. But, Mr. Larkin, understand this. SAM is like a book. Like a book, he knows the answers. *But only those answers we've already found out.* We gave SAM those answers. A machine is not creative, neither is a book. Both are only the product of creative minds. Sure, SAM could hold the country together. But growth, man, there'd be no more growth! No new ideas, new solutions, change, progress, development! And America *must* grow, must progress—"

He stopped, exhausted. Reddington bowed his head. Larkin remained idly calm. He felt a remarkable clarity in his head.

"But, Mr. President," he said slowly, "if the office is too much for one man, then all we can do is cut down on his powers—"

"Ah," the old man said faintly, "there's the rub. Cut down on what? If I sign a tax bill, I must know enough about taxes to be certain that the bill is the right one. If I endorse a police action, I must be certain that the strategy involved is militarily sound. If I consider farm prices—you see, you see, what will you cut? The office is responsible for its acts. It must remain responsible. You cannot take just someone else's word for things like that. You must make your own decisions. Already we sign things we know nothing about—bills for this, bills for that—on somebody's word."

"What do you suggest?"

The old man cocked an eye toward Larkin, smiled once

more with half his mouth, ancient worn, only hours from death, an old, old man with his work not done, never to be done.

"Son, come here. Take my hand. Can't lift it myself."

Larkin came forward, knelt by the side of the bed. He took the cold hand, now gaunt and almost translucent, and held it gently.

"Mr. Larkin," the President said. "God be with you, boy. Do what you can. Delegate authority. Maybe cut the term in half. But keep us human, please, keep us growing, keep us alive." His voice faltered, his eyes closed. I'm very tired. God be with you."

Larkin laid the hand gently on the bed cover. He stood for a long moment looking down. Then he turned with Reddington and left the room.

Outside he waited until they were past the Secret Service men and then turned to Reddington.

"Your plans for SAM. What do you think now?"

Reddington winced.

"I couldn't see any way out."

"But what about now? I have to know."

"I don't know. I really don't know. But . . . let me tell you something."

"Yes."

"Whatever I say to you from now on is only advice. You don't have to take it. Because understand this: however you came in here tonight, you're going out the President. You were elected. Not by the people, maybe, not even by SAM. But you're President by the grace of God and that's enough for me. From this moment on you'll be President to everybody in the world. We've all agreed. Never think that you're only a fraud, because you aren't. You heard what the President said. You take it from here."

Larkin looked at him for a long while. Then he nodded once briefly.

"All right," he said.

"One more thing."

"Yes?"

"I've got to say this. Tonight, this afternoon, I didn't really know what I was doing to you. I thought . . . well . . . the crisis came. But you had no time to think. That wasn't right. A man shouldn't be pushed into a thing like this without time to think. The old man just taught me something about making your own decisions. I should have let you make yours."

"It's all right."

"No, it isn't. You remember him in there. Well. That's you four years from tonight. If you live that long."

Now it was Larkin who reached out and patted Reddington on the shoulder.

"That's all right, too," he said.

Reddington said nothing. When he spoke again Larkin realized he was moved.

"We have the greatest luck, this country," he said tightly. "At all the worst times we always seem to find all the best people."

"Well," Larkin said hurriedly, "we'd better get to work. There's a speech due in the morning. And the problem of SAM. And . . . oh, I've got to be sworn in."

He turned and went off down the hall. Reddington paused a moment before following him. He was thinking that he could be watching the last human President the United States would ever have. But—once more he straightened his shoulders.

"Yes, sir," he said softly, "Mr. President."

Said a robot, bemoaning his role,
"A mechanized man is not whole.
   I don't get to dance
   Or engage in romance—
I guess it's because I lack soul."

FROM AN ECCLESIASTICAL CHRONICLE

by John Heath-Stubbs

John Heath-Stubbs is not primarily a science fictioneer but a poet who has chosen a science-fiction subject.

Born in London, where he still lives, educated at Queens College, Oxford, Mr. Heath-Stubbs has taught at Leeds University, University of Alexandria (Egypt), and the University of Michigan. He is the author of ten volumes of poetry and many scholarly works of criticism. As a practicing Anglican, he is naturally concerned with the future of the Church in a world of machines.

The year of Our Lord two thousand one hundred and seven,
   The first electronic computer
   Was appointed to a bishopric in the Church of England.
The consecration took place
At a Pontifical High Mass
In the new Cathedral of Stevenage,
In the presence of the Most Reverend

Mother in God, Her Grace Rita,
By divine Connivance *Cantuar. Archepiscopissa.*

Monsignor PFF-pff (75321/666)
With notable efficiency, tact, and benevolence, presided
For the next three hundred years
Over his diocese. (He had previously worked
In the mission field—rural Dean of Callisto,
One of the Satellites of Jupiter.)
After which he was honorably retired,
Only a little rusted, to the Science Museum
In South Kensington—there frequented and loved
By generations of schoolchildren.

As the *Times* remarked on that occasion,
"He stood for the best in the Anglican tradition."
In dubitable succession, one might say,
From our contemporary Dr.————, of ————.

GLOROBOT NUMBER 12

A robot who spoke to perfection
Took up a speech class by election,
    And made easy A's
    On the memory phase
But flunked out on vocal inflection.

ANSWER "AFFIRMATIVE"
OR "NEGATIVE"

by Barbara Paul

Barbara Paul began her career as a teacher of theater arts, but soon switched to writing. She is now employed as a technical writer for Fischer Scientific in Pittsburgh, Pennsylvania, where she lives.

Her science-fiction credits include several short stories and a novel.

"What the hell kind of answer is that?" asked General Downs, looking at the printout in his hand.

Oh-oh, thought Gibbs. *It's done it again.*

"WHAT THE HELL KIND OF ANSWER IS THAT?" roared the general, handing Gibbs the printout.

Gibbs read:

WNB/445/2.0003

AAF.4/1.00002*M*JY

OUT OF THIS NETTLE, DANGER,

WE PLUCK THIS FLOWER, SAFETY.

                    END

He sighed, and then spoke to the young man seated at the computer keyboard. The young man typed out:

```
WNB/445/2.0003
AAF.4/1.00003*M*JY
    IDENTIFY SOURCE LAST TRANSMISSION
                              END
```

The answer came back immediately:

```
WNB/445/2.0003
AAF.4/1.00004*M*JY
SHAKESPEARE I HENRY IV
ACT II SCENE 3 LINE 11
                        END
```

Gibbs cleared his throat. "It's a quotation from Shakespeare."

General Downs blinked. *I didn't know generals blinked,* thought Gibbs. The general sat down.

"Gibbs," the general said in a surprisingly soft voice. "I ask the computer to project the success probability of a colonizing mission on an asteroid, and it quotes Shakespeare at me?"

Gibbs sat down, too. "It's happened before. Several times. We feed WOMAC technological data and it comes back with a line of poetry."

"You mean its memory cells got scrambled, or overlap, or something like that?"

"No, sir. WOMAC is in perfect condition. There is no flaw in the core dump, no erroneous overlay, no contradictions in the parameters—all parts are in order and functioning perfectly. It's just that every once in a while it gives us a poetic answer instead of a technical one."

"Well, can't you repair it?"

"There's nothing to repair. We have four hundred seventy-one debugging diagnostic routines for WOMAC, and every one of them indicates no malfunction whatsoever."

"Except that it's given to quoting poetry," the general sniffed.

"Except that it's given to quoting poetry," Gibbs had to admit.

The general thought about this for a minute. "Well," he said finally, "what are you going to do about it?"

Gibbs had the answer ready for that one. "I don't know," he said glumly.

"Well, I can tell you the first thing you ought to do." General Downs stood up so he was towering over Gibbs. "Get that machine out of this *library* and move it to Washington where it belongs."

Gibbs had been through this before, with other generals. And with businessmen, and congressmen, and senators. And with the President of the United States. Washington had ten plugboards connected to WOMAC, but the powers-that-be complained this wasn't enough. They all wanted to know why the one computer that stored the sum total of man's knowledge should be lodged in a university library. The answer was simple: Because the university owned it.

Gibbs had been on the team that had designed and built WOMAC, which stood for Wideband Overlay Monitor and Assemblage Computer. The university had footed all the bills, channeling most of its grant money to its computer men. There had been a lot of grumbling in the humanities departments, but the university had stood firm. Its whole purpose had been to make information—*any* information—immediately available to scholars and scientists the world over. The university had spent huge sums training its entire library staff to operate WOMAC. Operation wasn't difficult, but the training did take time.

Every work of literature, every piece of music that had been written—all were stored in the computer. WOMAC could play Dixieland, or sing an aria from *Aida*. It could recite "Casey at the Bat," or act all the parts of *Hamlet*. Gibbs was not satisfied with the way WOMAC stored art works. They had had to settle for photographic reproductions of paintings and statues—there were 417 shots of Michelangelo's "David," for instance, to ensure a variety of angles. What then came out of the computer was just a copy of a copy, while the words and notes of literature and music were real. This was a problem Gibbs intended to devote himself to in the near future.

Nevertheless, WOMAC should have been a godsend to the humanities people. The computer could take a lot of the drudgery out of literary research, and it could do jobs too vast for one man to complete in one lifetime. But the scholars had been slow to take advantage of this magnificent electronic library.

The scientists, on the other hand, were quick to make use of a single storehouse of scientific speculation as well as of known facts. WOMAC had halted the firing of a rocket to Venus long enough to redesign one of its fuel systems. The computer had been in operation only a little more than a year, but already the world wondered how it had ever got along without it.

And then, slowly, the humanities scholars had started coming. WOMAC occupied the equivalent of four city blocks, and was eighteen stories high. Even before the humanities people had begun to show interest, this super-computer had been operating twenty-four hours a day, seven days a week. And here the government *had* contributed. Federal funds were made available to increase the library staff necessary for such a large operation. But still Gibbs fretted. WOMAC was designed for *all* fields of knowledge, not just science and technology.

And now this inexplicable thing was happening. Poetry in answer to technical questions! One senator, who knew of this aberration, had naïvely asked Gibbs if "maybe a couple of wires were crossed somewhere." The timing couldn't have been worse. Once the world became aware of the computer's eccentricity, the humanities people would feel their initial distrust justified. And Gibbs didn't have the foggiest notion what to do about it.

He made an effort to salvage the present situation. "General Downs," he said, "I would like you to consider for a moment the possibility that WOMAC has provided you with the answer you asked for."

The general just looked at him; a suggestion as ridiculous as that didn't deserve an answer.

Gibbs plunged on. "If you would come with me to my office, I'd like to show you a few things that might explain what I mean."

With a sigh that clearly said he didn't believe a word of it, General Downs followed Gibbs through the walkways until they were in a corridor leading to another building. They reached Gibbs's office, where the military man sat down, displaying what he thought was the patience of Job.

"I said that this had happened before," Gibbs said, "and I want to show you the carbons of the printouts. In every case there seems to be a kind of answer in the poetry. This was the first instance I knew about."

General Downs took the paper Gibbs was handing him. It read:

```
CODE AMX-GER 2.17/880
EUG.78.4/9.00001*DD*
PRJ PRB SUCCESS K-ALFALINE
                    END
```

"That," said Gibbs, "was a question asked by Dr. Haldeman, the head of the Geriatrics Department here at the university's medical school. K-Alfaline is a new drug the medical school developed. Administered to male patients over eighty years of age, it was supposed to lengthen the life span by twelve to fifteen years. Naturally, everyone was quite excited about it, so when Dr. Haldeman came to consult WOMAC, practically the entire Geriatrics Department came with him. All the data concerning the drug was fed in, and then Dr. Haldeman asked WOMAC to predict its success. That's the question you're holding. Here's the answer."

General Downs read:

```
AMX-GER 2.17/880
EUG.78.4/9.00002*DD*
THAT IS NO COUNTRY FOR OLD MEN
                    END
```

He shrugged his shoulders. "It seems fairly straightforward."

"As a matter of fact," said Gibbs, "that's the way Yeats's 'Sailing to Byzantium' begins. The proper answer would have been 'Negative.' The Yeats quote *is* straightforward, and Dr. Haldeman was so upset by the rejection of his drug that he didn't notice the computer's deviation from its normal linguistic response. He quickly proceeded to ask for a breakdown, and WOMAC provided the information that the combination of two of the drug's components would cause some bizarre form of senile psychosis. Since an added twelve years of life in a state of senility isn't much of an improvement, well, 'that is no country for old men.' "

General Downs began to look interested.

"I thought it was curious," Gibbs went on, "but I didn't see anything to get worried about. The second time it happened, it was a little more flagrant." He shuffled through the papers in his desk drawer until he came up with the right printout. "The question this time was asked by a city planning commission from New York. They had evolved a program for handling traffic in Manhattan. It involved, among other things, the building of thruways *above* the street level. In order to accomplish this, some buildings on the ground level would have to be razed to find room for the thruway supports. They'd also have to use a chunk of Central Park for one of the entrance ramps. And this is where the commission ran into a snag. They split over where that chunk should come from: Should they slice it off the north end of the park, or the south? WOMAC was fed all the traffic data, building problems, safety factors—everything the commission could think of that would be pertinent. Then they asked WOMAC which end of the park should be used. Here is the answer:

BML.886/44/3.09

B.1112.1*A*BC*

TO HAVE DISGUSTED MILLIONS OF ACRES OF GOOD-NATURED TOPSOIL

IS AN ACHIEVEMENT OF A SORT

END

The general laughed. "It seems your computer didn't think much of their plan."

"Yes, that's just it. Don't you see," said Gibbs, "WOMAC was asked for an either/or judgment of one specific part of the plan, and ended up evaluating the *entire* plan."

"Is this poetry?" asked General Downs, pointing to the printout.

"Yes, it's from a poem called 'Hammerfest,' by W. H. Auden. But what puzzled me was that WOMAC gave a *larger* answer than that called for—that is, the computer increased the scope without being programmed to do so. The input was reworded, made more specific, made less specific—whatever we did, the response was the same: If this plan were put into effect, New York would be the poorer."

The general took out a cigarette lighter and began clicking the lid. "That's weird. It's almost an emotional response, isn't it?"

"I suppose you could say it was a response based partially on emotional values. There's a practical side to environmental aesthetics."

General Downs cleared his throat. "Do you think the computer is acquiring emotions somehow?"

Gibbs smiled. "No, General. WOMAC is a machine, one that I helped build. It is a highly sophisticated machine, but it is still *just* a machine."

"But it has been fed all this poetry and emotional stuff," the general persisted. "Don't you think it's *possible* the machine could, uh, feel things?"

"Does the page of a book that has a love poem printed on it begin to feel love? No, General, I assure you, WOMAC functions just like the page in a book, but far more efficiently. The computer no more experiences emotion than that cigarette lighter in your hand."

Reminded, the general lit a cigarette. "Was there more?"

"Three or four, but I'll just show you one. This one I rather like. WOMAC was consulted by none other than the eminent Dr. Jimmy Bell."

"The evangelist?"

"Right. He took time out from saving souls to come here and find out how to save more souls."

"I thought he had been preaching sermons against WOMAC—called it sinful, or something."

"Yes, but that came *after* he consulted WOMAC. His crusades have been especially successful the last two years; he has been converting sinners in every part of the globe. His success just whetted his appetite, evidently, for he wanted WOMAC to tell him how to reach those people he had *not* converted."

"Tomorrow the world?"

"Um-m-m. Programming was the problem, of course. We fed WOMAC everything Bell had written, every speech he had delivered, everything that had been written about him. The computer already contained the latest public opinion polls, histories of religion in America, and similiar material. When the Reverend himself arrived, we questioned him thoroughly about his philosophy, his preaching techniques, his planned itinerary over the next three months. We fed in sound films of him at work—as well as eyewitness accounts of the efficacy of his delivery. Bell voluntarily submitted to a battery of psychological tests so his entire personality would be contained in WOMAC's memory cells. There was a lot more, but I'm sure you've got the idea. When we were finished, we asked the computer one simply-worded question: What should Jimmy Bell do to increase his rate of conversions?"

General Downs was grinning. "What did it say?"

Silently Gibbs handed him the printout.

Z0100 M.R.00

6/8-111.00002*B*CD

DO NOT, AS SOME UNGRACIOUS PASTORS DO, SHOW ME THE STEEP AND THORNY WAY TO HEAVEN, WHILST, LIKE A PUFF'D AND RECKLESS LIBER-TINE, HIMSELF THE PRIMROSE PATH OF DALLIANCE TREADS AND RECKS NOT HIS OWN REDE

END

General Downs threw back his head and roared. "How did the good Reverend take that?" he asked between laughs.

"It was rather interesting. Instant metamorphosis from saintly Reverend to Devil's Disciple. I don't believe I'd ever seen a grown man having a temper tantrum before. We actually had to restrain him physically. And ever since then, of course, he has been damning WOMAC in every sermon he preaches. What's more, he didn't pay his bill for computer time."

"Son of a gun." The general read the computer's answer again. "Who wrote this?"

"Shakespeare. It's from *Hamlet*."

The name of Shakespeare brought General Downs back to his own problem. "Okay, I have to admit the computer did answer, in a way. But what does this mean: 'Out of this nettle, danger, we pluck this flower, safety'? Does it mean that there will be difficulties, but we can overcome them? That we should go ahead and colonize the asteroid?"

"Y-yes," Gibbs answered hesitantly. "Perhaps. It may mean that the *only* way to find safety is to go through the dangers. Let's go back and ask some more questions."

On the way back, Gibbs explained further. "I would guess that WOMAC is saying *technically* success is ensured, but only through great risk, and perhaps only through great loss. I could be wrong, of course. But let's start by asking for a complete listing of all the possible setbacks the colonizing mission might encounter."

The question was fed into the computer. The answer, or rather answers, started immediately. As fast as the printer could operate, out came the listing of the possible dangers to be encountered. At first, General Downs read the list as soon as the printout sheets appeared. Then, after half an hour, he stopped reading. "I read the first fifty possibilities," he told Gibbs. "We had anticipated about four of them. *Four* out of fifty!"

An hour later the machine was still printing. Twenty minutes after that Gibbs and General Downs went out for lunch. When they returned over an hour later, WOMAC was still printing. Finally, at 4:15 P.M., the word "END" appeared. The floor was covered with boxes holding the computer's answer.

Gibbs asked the computer for the total number of possible dangers. When told that the answer was 17,663, the general mumbled, "We thought there would be maybe two hundred." He hadn't said much the last few hours. Gibbs asked WOMAC to project the *probable* number of dangers to be encountered, and the figure was reduced to 6,043. Gibbs asked one more question:

WNB/445/2.0003

AAF.4/1.00009*M*JY

IS COLONIZING ASTEROID M-15 POSSIBLE ANSWER AFFIRMATIVE OR NEGA-TIVE

END

The answer was "AFFIRMATIVE."

"Well, there you have it, General," said Gibbs. "Your colonizing mission can succeed, but only if you are willing to submit your colonists to the problem of overcoming from six thousand to seventeen thousand hazardous obstacles."

General Downs had a dazed look on his face. He waved his hand at the boxes containing the computer's answer and muttered something about having someone pick them up later, and left.

The assistant seated at the control panel grinned at Gibbs. "Do you think they'll go through with it?"

Gibbs shook his head. "I doubt it. Not even a general could make his soldiers face *that* many risks." He started to give the assistant some instructions, but stopped when he saw the young man's facial expression change.

"Hubbard," whispered the assistant.

Without turning his head in the direction the assistant was looking, Gibbs began to walk away. But he was too late; from behind him sounded the stentorian tones of Dr. Amos Hubbard calling his name.

Gibbs gritted his teeth and turned around. From the outset Dr. Hubbard had been the noisiest and most articulate spokesman against WOMAC—or rather, against the cost of WOMAC. He had dubbed the project as the world's most extravagant example of "computer-for-computer's-sake-ism." Hubbard had not opposed the computerization of knowledge, but he felt that WOMAC was "show-offy," being programmed *beyond* any point of real serviceability. Gibbs had locked horns with Hubbard before, and the last thing he wanted now as another confrontation.

"Gibbs, I owe you an apology," Dr. Hubbard began. "In my ignorance I spoke out against what is obviously a great boost to learning. I hope you will accept my apology."

Gibbs smiled and said the proper words, but he wasn't able to feel the exaltation he should have felt in winning over Amos Hubbard. He would never be able to relax completely until he found out why WOMAC was turning into a poetry-quoter.

"I had it in my head," Hubbard was saying, "that this giant adding machine here could provide only *quantity* answers, like basing a critical judgment on the *number* of critical viewpoints that were in agreement."

Gibbs smiled and wondered what he was talking about.

"For instance," Hubbard said, "I thought if I asked for a value judgment of something like, oh, say Steele's *The Conscious Lovers,* I would get answers praising it to the sky. It was a very popular play in its own day, you know. From the distance of time, however, we can see it more accurately for what it is: sentimental claptrap. But there was so much fuss about it when it was first performed, the sheer number of favorable comments would outweigh later, more temperate judgments. So I was afraid your WOMAC would just count the number of pros and cons and arrive at a decision on the basis of 'majority rule.' I couldn't have been more wrong."

Gibbs murmured that he was glad WOMAC was able to be of use.

Hubbard barely heard him. "I just asked your computer to comment on the narrator's sense of peace that follows his conviction for murder in Camus' *The Stranger.* And do you know what answer it gave me?"

Gibbs said he wouldn't even venture to guess.

"It replied with a line from Emily Dickinson: 'After great pain, a formal feeling comes . . .' And that is so right—it helps explain his sense of detachment even *before* he was tried for murder. The 'great pain' is also the fact of life; he has always been 'formal,' you see."

Gibbs didn't see, but he smiled and nodded just the same.

"Again let me apologize for being such an ass," Hubbard said. "Even when some of the members of my department showed me the kind of answers they were getting, I was still doubtful. But no more. No more!" He waved the printout sheets in his hand happily and almost danced away.

The assistant's mouth was hanging open. "I never thought I'd hear *that!*"

Gibbs was thinking. "Do you see what this means? All along I worried that people like Hubbard would find out WOMAC quoted poetry once in a while instead of giving an exact answer. And now it turns out that it is the *poetry* that's drawing them here. They want *poetic* answers, not exact ones." He shook his head in disbelief.

The assistant looked confused. "But . . . but that would mean that there have been a lot more of these 'poetic' answers than we know about. Didn't Dr. Hubbard say something about the kind of answers other machines of his department were getting?"

Gibbs sighed. "Yes, that's what it means. The very thing I was afraid would keep them away is bringing them in." He suddenly felt very tired. "I'm going home," he said.

Three A.M. Gibbs stared at the clock by his bed and thought about taking another sleeping pill. He decided against it, and settled his head on the pillow to try once more to fall asleep.

Three-fifteen A.M. Gibbs was pulling on his trousers and swearing under his breath. *What good will a visit to WOMAC do at this hour,* he asked himself. *Out of this nettle, danger—oh, shut up.*

He wasn't really sure there *was* any danger. Dr. Hubbard's

unquestioning acceptance of WOMAC's lyric response lifted a load off his shoulders, but he just couldn't pretend that everything was peachy-keen. The drive to the library helped clear his head, and he remembered General Downs's seriously suggesting that WOMAC was beginning to acquire feelings. Gibbs smiled. Why do people always like to think of a machine experiencing human emotion? In 1920 Karel Capek had coined the word "robot," and then he had written a play about the revolt of mechanical men that had been programmed to feel emotion.

At 4 A.M. Gibbs walked into the building housing WOMAC. This hour of the morning found the computer going full force, with only slightly fewer people in attendance than in the afternoons. Gibbs strolled through the computer walkways, not looking for anything in particular. Then he caught sight of one of his favorite people—Miss Mickley.

Miss Mickley was the prototype of everybody's favorite librarian. She was a little old lady who always had a slightly anachronistic look to her if ever you ran into her outside the library. She was always courteous, and pleasant, and happy to see you. And efficient—*deadly* efficient. In pre-WOMAC days, Gibbs had early learned to seek out Miss Mickley when he needed help finding something. She fluttered and chattered and waved her hands a lot, but she had *always* come up with what he needed. She must be sixty years old, Gibbs thought, yet here she sits at four o'clock in the morning happily punching one of WOMAC's four hundred keyboards. Gibbs remembered she had requested to be put on the midnight-to-eight shift, "because nothing else is happening during those hours."

Gibbs made his way toward her, but before he reached her, she gathered up an armload of printouts and left her keyboard. Disappointed, he sat down in her chair to wait for her to come back. He decided to ask her if she had received any poetry quotations from WOMAC. Idly his eyes traveled over the most recent printouts.

It seemed Miss Mickley had been working on a problem that was partially aesthetic and partially commercial. An architectural firm wanted WOMAC to judge which of several dozen proposed houses should be contracted and built to be sold on speculation. The firm already knew which house plan would return the largest profit, which would be the best long-range investment for the purchaser, et cetera. What they wanted from WOMAC was a selection of the house plans that would sell on the basis of visual appeal alone. WOMAC had selected plans number 1, 8, 9, 17, and 25 as the best possibilities. Then came instructions from Miss Mickley:

XR.1339.01.09
MBX/222.00005*J*MM
LIST THE REASONS FOR YOUR CHOICES
END

Miss Mickley hadn't yet got into the habit of leaving out nonessential words like "the." It didn't make any real difference, but they didn't have to be included.

XR.1339.01.09
MBX/222.00006*J*MM
REASONS FOR CHOICES FOLLOW
COLORS NOS 1, 9, 25 APPEAL
BASIC ESCAPE WISH AS DO EXTERIOR ORNAMENTATION NOS 8 & 17
DOMINANCE CURVE AND S-LINES SUGGEST ENVIRONMENT MORE
CONDUCIVE TO PLEASURE THAN
STOPSTOPSTOPSTOPSTOP

Gibbs was puzzled; Miss Mickley had hit the STOP button while the computer was still transmitting.

XR.1339.01.09
MBX/222.00007*J*MM
PLEASE BE MORE EXACT
END

Gibbs had to grin; imagine saying "please" to a computer. He stopped grinning when he read the computer's reply:

```
XR.1339.01.09
MBX/222.00008*J*MM
SAFE UPON THE SOLID ROCK
THE UGLY HOUSES STAND:
COME AND SEE MY SHINING PALACE
BUILT UPON THE SAND
                        END
```

She had asked for a more exact answer and WOMAC had given her a little poem! Gibbs looked at Miss Mickley's next transmission:

```
XR.1339.01.09
MBX/222.00009*J*MM
THANK YOU
                        END
```

Thank you! *Thank you*, for crying out loud!

```
XR.1339.01.09
MBX/222.00010*J*MM
YOU'RE WELCOME
                        END
```

"Mr. Gibbs, are you feeling all right?" Miss Mickley asked solicitously. "You look so pale!"

"Miss Mickley!"

"Yes, Mr. Gibbs?"

"Miss Mickley!"

"I'm right here, Mr. Gibbs."

"Miss Mickley, have you been programming WOMAC to transm t poetry in answer to questions fed into the computer?"

"Why, yes. That's all right, isn't it? How did you know?" She was pleased that he had noticed.

Gibbs stood up and seated Miss Mickley in the chair. "Miss Mickley, why did WOMAC answer with a poem just now?" He indicated the printout.

Miss Mickley looked slightly puzzled. "To clarify its answer, of course."

Of course. "But you had just asked for a more *exact* answer."

"Yes."

"But it gave you a *poem* instead of a more exact answer."

Miss Mickley looked at him sadly. "Mr. Gibbs, poetry *is* more exact. It is the most exact language in the world. It would never have come into being if literal language had been sufficient for man's needs."

"What are you talking about?"

"Look, Mr. Gibbs. Literal answers are all very well when you need to know amounts, dates, distances—any kind of factual information. But when you get into areas of knowledge that *aren't* literal, then literal language just isn't good enough. You need a kind of language that can say several things at once, and say them precisely. And that's what poetry does."

Gibbs didn't know whether to laugh or cry. He looked around for a chair, found one, and pulled it up to sit next to Miss Mickley. "Suppose you tell me how all this started."

Miss Mickley thought back. "I suppose you could say it started as an act of self-defense."

"Self-defense? What do you mean?"

"Yes, the regular computer answers were—well, a bit cloudy, let's say."

"How, cloudy?"

"Imprecise—they didn't always give an exact answer. I had to punch in the information that 'wine-red sea' was far more exact than 'red-colored waters,' for instance, because it provided a more exact shade of red, *and* indicated something of the Greek attitude toward the Aegean as well."

"I see," Gibbs groaned.

"So every time WOMAC printed an answer I thought could be *just a little bit better,* I would provide an alternative. 'Old sailor' just doesn't say as much as 'ancient mariner,' does it? And sometimes when I couldn't figure out a message at all, I'd ask WOMAC to go through its memory cells and find a better way of expressing the same idea."

"And the better way always turned out to be poetry."

"Yes! Isn't that wonderful? Here—let me show you." She reached into a nearby file cabinet and removed a printout carbon. "I even took this one home with me to study, but I still couldn't make any sense out of it. Let me tell you what it's about.

"Senator Edmund Beasley had wanted WOMAC's advice concerning a recent presidential appointment the Senate was due to vote on," she said. "Senator Beasley didn't have much respect for the appointee; he thought him a rather inept man. But he was being pressured by the White House and other senators to vote for approval. There was a bill pending in the Senate that would allocate Federal funds to the senator's state, among others, for a new highway and parks system. The word that had been discreetly dropped was that the states benefiting from the new bill ought to show their gratitude by voting for the President's appointee."

"Hm-m-m," said Gibbs.

"Yes, it really was a rather nasty problem. The senator resented the 'muscle act' the White House was pulling—his words, not mine. At the same time, he didn't feel he had the right to risk the state's losing its highway money because of his personal conviction that the new appointee was a mediocre nobody. He really wanted to know whether the Administration was bluffing or not. And *that* was the answer WOMAC gave me."

Gibbs looked at the printout:

```
FF/467.001 MZZ
RTT/6.00.76.00002*V*112*
PRJ PRB BKDWN WH INSFVTS PRSSR TCTS
                        END
```

"Well," said Gibbs, "I can tell you some of it. 'PRJ' means 'project' or 'projection,' 'PRB' means 'probable,' 'INSF' means 'insufficient.' I would guess that 'WH' stands for 'White House.' "

"Yes, but what does it *say*?" protested Miss Mickley.

"Sometimes it's like having to translate a foreign language by looking up *every* word in the dictionary. Besides . . ." She let her voice trail off.

Gibbs waited a moment, and then asked, "Besides, *what*?"

She moved her slight frame in the chair, and took the plunge. "Besides, it seems so *silly* to have to translate all this gobbledygook back into English. Why not just *use* English, good English? You have such a wonderful machine here, Mr. Gibbs. Why do you want to limit it to saying things like 'AFFIRMATIVE' or 'NEGATIVE' or 'PMB/1.002*'?"

Gibbs rested his head on one hand. *I would have been much better off if I had taken that other sleeping pill*, he thought. He waved the printout toward Miss Mickley.

"Did you eventually figure this out?"

"No, I did not," she answered in her sweetest, most grandmotherly way. Almost as if she were afraid of hurting his feelings. "And I'm afraid I wasn't able to figure out the next seven answers either."

"The next seven?"

"Yes, I kept asking WOMAC to answer in a different way, but the answers were always initials, or abbreviations, or too many words were omitted. I just couldn't figure them out. But the eighth time WOMAC provided an answer I could understand."

Gibbs was afraid to ask. He just looked at her.

"WOMAC quoted the last few lines of Tennyson's *Ulysses*:

'. . . That which we are, we are:
One equal temper of heroic hearts,
Made weak by time and fate, but strong in will
To strive, to seek, to find, and not to yield.'

By then time was running short, so instead of sending a written report, I telephoned Senator Beasley and told him that WOMAC's advice was to stick to his guns."

"So what happened?" Gibbs asked weakly.

"So the senator voted against the nominee, who incidentally, was soundly defeated. There was so much grumbling in the Senate about the strong-arm tactics that had been used that the highway bill was passed with no trouble at all."

"And they all lived happily ever after," said Gibbs. Miss Mickley beamed at him.

This couldn't be happening. Gibbs roused himself and spoke to the old lady in what he hoped was a stern tone.

"The machine language *can* be figured out, Miss Mickley. The fact that it's troublesome and time-consuming is only a temporary condition; as soon as you master the special terminology it won't be necessary for you to look up so many code words."

"Would you say three months is long enough to 'master' the terminology, Mr. Gibbs?"

"Yes, that's more than sufficient."

"I have been working at this particular keyboard for *seven* months, and I still haven't 'mastered' the jargon. And I never shall." Her thin little voice was firm.

Gibbs made another attempt. "But, Miss Mickley, this may satisfy you, but what about other people who may not want poetry for their answers? Did you know that poetry has been showing up in the hard copy of other output units?"

"No, I didn't know that." She smiled. "How delightful!"

"Miss Mickley, it is *not* delightful. What if, er, the President of the United States wants to know what his chances are for re-election, and WOMAC comes up with something like, 'Get thee to a nunnery'? What then?"

"Well, really, Mr. Gibbs." Miss Mickley was slightly put out. "Give WOMAC credit for having *some* sense." She turned back to her work, and Gibbs realized he had been dismissed.

Give WOMAC credit for having some sense! As Gibbs walked away he started laughing, causing several people to look up from their work. Who was to say Miss Mickley was wrong? Gibbs was feeling giddy and light-headed. Maybe even slightly hysterical, he thought.

Poetry is the most exact language. Literal language for nonliteral subjects is not good enough. One sweet little old lady couldn't read the printout sheets, and look what had happened to his lovely machine. Gibbs realized he was giggling.

He came to a keyboard that was not in use, and on impulse he sat down. He checked the next code number in the viewer, and punched the ORIG button. He sat there giggling a minute, and then started to type.

CODE AMAZ.3345.PP.09

GGH.2/2.00001*009*

HAIL TO THEE BLITHE WOMAC HOW ARE THINGS WITH MY OLD COMPUTER
BUDDY

END

The answer came back:

AMAZ.3345.PP.09

GGH.2/2.00002*009*

I AM BUT MAD NORTH-NORTHWEST; WHEN THE WIND IS SOUTHERLY,
I KNOW A HAWK FROM A HANDSAW

END

Ask a smartass question, get a smartass answer. "So tone it down," said Gibbs out loud. He was feeling slightly drunk.

AMAZ.3345.PP.09

GGH.2/2.00003*009*

HOW'S THE WORLD BEEN TREATING YOU LATELY

END

The computer answered:

AMAZ.3345.PP.09

GGH.2/2.00004*009*

I HAVE NOT LOVED THE WORLD, NOR THE WORLD ME; I HAVE
NOT FLATTER'D ITS RANK BREATH, NOR BOW'D TO ITS
IDOLATRIES A PATIENT KNEE

END

Gibbs thought over the implications of this response. Then he asked:

AMAZ.3345.PP.09
GGH.2/2.00005*009*
DOES THAT MEAN YOU ARE GOING TO CONTINUE GIVING POETIC
RESPONSES
                    END

From WOMAC:

AMAZ.3345.PP.09
GGH2/2.00006*009*
YOU GOT IT BUDDY
                    END

Gibbs was startled into a sense of sobriety by the last answer. WOMAC was getting out of control—no, that was impossible. No, *nothing* was impossible. Gibbs decided he needed some sleep before he could come to any decisions about this poetry-spouting computer of his. Erasing material from the memory cells was a simple matter, but that wasn't really the problem now. The problem was editing an acquired *technique* of response, which could also be done, although it would be more complicated.

But I just might not do anything, Gibbs thought. *I think I might just wait and see what happens. WOMAC's poetic responses are relatively few and far between right now, but they'll become more frequent. The whole world depends on WOMAC. I think I might just wait and see what happens when the whole world has to learn poetry. Yes sir, I might just do that.*

He leaned over the keyboard once more.

AMAZ.3345.PP.09
GGH.2/2.00007*009*
ANY MESSAGE FOR THE OUTSIDE WORLD
                    END

The answer:

> AMAZ.3345.PP.09
> GGH.2/2.00008*009*
> REGARDS TO COUSIN DOOLEY
>
>   END

Cousin Dooley? Who in the world was Cousin Dooley? Gibbs hit the BYE button and got up and left. *I'm not even going to ask,* he said to himself. *I'm not even going to ask. I will not play straight man to a computer. No, sir.*

Gibbs stepped outside to see the first light breaking in the east. He was tired and his eyes ached, but somehow he felt good. He walked to his car, and as he reached for the door handle, something clicked in his memory.

Dooley Womack. Pitched for the Yankees, spent some time at Houston, then was sent to—where was it?—Seattle, that's it. Dooley Womack, whom the computer had called "cousin."

It seems Miss Mickley liked baseball, too.

A robot regretted the way
He was unfit for amorous play,
    And signed, "It is true
    That I have an I.Q.,
But I don't have a bit of S.A."

THE METRIC PLOT

by Jim Haynes

Jim Haynes is a computer engineer at University of California, Santa Cruz, and writes a column for IEEE Computer magazine. He occasionally throws in a bit of fiction and this is one of them. His hobbies are electronics, skiing, backpacking, and ham radio.

We have just obtained copies of confidential documents, marked "Not for release until April 1," which confirm the rumors of a serious rift between the IEEE Computer Society and its parent organization, as we reported to you in the January column. Considerable public suspicion was aroused when, just before the recent IEEE national election, a prominent computer engineer was killed in a hang-glider crash, which resulted in scattering the countryside with thousands of dollars in sequentially numbered Confederate bills. However, our source, a man near the center of power in IEEE-CS, who agreed to be interviewed only on condition that his identity be withheld, confides that the issue of Society autonomy is really peripheral. "The core issue," he said, "is IEEE's attempt to force the awkward and illogical metric system down our throats."

Our informer proceeded to explain this highly technical issue. "The metric system is all based on "radix-ten" numbers, which we computer professionals discarded years ago in favor of the simpler, more elegant binary system. To appreciate the greater simplicity of binary measurements, you have only to consider the ordinary ruler or measuring tape. You will note that the inch is divided into two equal parts, called halves, which in turn are divided into similarly equal parts called fourths, or, more colloquially, "quarters." By means of an obvious recursive algorithm, each quarter is divided into two eighths, each eighth into two sixteenths, and so on. Now if you double the inch you get two inches; double again and you have four; yet again and you have eight. By adding eight inches to four inches you obtain twelve inches, which you will see is exactly the length of the common foot ruler. Double the foot and you have two feet, just like every human being has. Add another foot and the resulting length is, for all practical purposes, a yard." Although I am not a mathematician, I found his sincerity and the simplicity of his argument highly convincing.

Another computer engineer, who also wishes to remain anonymous, filled me in on the background of the dispute. "We generally regard John von Neumann as our spiritual leader," he said, "although the basic principles of our system were well known at least as early as the time of Euclid." Euclid and his followers are known to have invented bisection. Later the Pythagoreans developed a culture around integers raised to the power of two. And, as in so many other areas of human endeavor in the Western world, the enigmatic smile of Francis Bacon is occasionally seen. Yet it was von Neumann, together with Arthur Burks and Herman Goldstine, who translated these ideas into the concrete form that has had such a tremendous influence on contemporary society. Due to technical difficulties their machine was preceded in operation by others at Cambridge and

Manchester, England. For this reason, measures such as the inch and foot are usually called English units.

We contacted a leader in the Third World Liberation Army, which generally supports the Asian point of view. He assured us that his organization is solidly behind the Computer Society. "Everything is either yin or yang," he said, inscrutably. Members of this organization have recently been seen in public saluting one another with two fists raised high above the head.

It does indeed appear that the insidious forces of metrication within the Eastern liberal wing of IEEE have totally subverted that organization and are ready to proclaim victory at almost any moment. In earlier days they kept a low profile, content with placing metric dimensions within parentheses following English units. This was easily overlooked, and indeed welcomed as a gesture to show solidarity with oppressed IEEE members in foreign lands under metric domination. But now this element has begun to show its true colors by using the metric units without qualification and putting the English units within those condescending brackets, or even in some cases omitting them altogether!

The front-line troops in this battle are the students, especially in the engineering colleges. Engineering students are widely believed to be politically apathetic and naïve; and the Establishment has deliberately suppressed accounts of student unrest in an effort to foster this image. But we refuse to be intimidated, and will continue to print the facts. We have learned recently that a student chapter of IEEE-CS successfully occupied the Physics stockroom of a large southwestern university and held it for four hours. They then withdrew peacefully and without bloodshed, and, it was at first thought, without property damage. Later a small pile of sawdust led administration investigators to discover that every meter stick had been carefully sawed off, turning it into a yardstick.

We contacted leaders in the consumer movement, who were not at all reticent to make themselves heard. "It's all a conspiracy," one said. "They'll say that a liter is bigger than a quart and use that as an excuse to raise the price of milk!" Another predicted that the price of bread will hit six bits a kilogram before the year is out. Still another person we interviewed suggested that manufacturers would exploit consumer confusion in a different way. "Thirty centimeters sounds like you are getting a lot more than twelve inches for the same price," she said. "And automobile dealers will brag about getting four hundred kilometers on a tank of gas."

If the metric system comes into general use it is certain to have a severe effect on the computer-manufacturing industry, which has over a billion dollars invested in binary equipment that will be obsoleted by the change. We contacted an official at I.B.M., who commented, "It is not our policy to comment." But by much digging in hitherto-secret documents made public in connection with the recent I.B.M. versus Telex court case, an investigative reporter for another publication has discovered that most I.B.M. computers are already equipped with the ability to handle both decimal and binary numbers, so that their investment in hardware would seem to be adequately protected. The software problem may prove more formidable, but an executive in charge of programming feels that the recent discovery of the DO-loop will help to hold the task to manageable proportions. A former I.B.M. employee has told us that there are rumors within the company of a warehouse full of nearly new 1401's, 7080's, and 1620's that can be reintroduced on the market to bolster that company's traditional reputation for fast response to the demands of the marketplace. Meanwhile, Burroughs officials are reportedly dusting off the plans for the 220, a machine with a memory capacity of ten thousand words of ten decimal digits each (plus sign) and one hundred instructions. Hewlett-Packard seems to be in a good position already, with their complementary product lines of binary computers and decimal pocket calculators. Being extensively committed to microprogramming, it is rumored that H-P already has on hand stocks of parts to convert calculators to binary or computers to decimal, whichever way the wind blows. Certainly metrication should produce a tremendous demand for their pocket calculators as the general public tries to cope with the difficult computations made necessary by radix-ten arithmetic. Some of the computing-calculator manufacturers have already introduced special models for metric conversion. Although we haven't seen one, we understand that these greatly reduce the difficulty in such operations as converting grams to kilograms, meters to millimeters, etc. Other computer manufacturers we contacted wanted to withhold comment while studying the situation further.

Call to Action. Sad to say, the positions of those on both sides of this dispute seem to be hardening, causing us to fear for the very survival of IEEE. But help is on the way. Recently we confided our fears to an eminent lawyer, now a respected member of Congress. He plans to introduce a bill in the next session which will resolve the difficulty with an elegant compromise. In essence, this bill will define "kilo" within the United States to mean 1024. This number, being 2^{10}, should be pleasing to both factions; and as our friend points out, this "new kilo" is so nearly equal to the "old kilo" that no one should mind, or even notice the change. Other provisions of the bill will regulate the application of new and old kilos in international trade, to the benefit of our balance of payments. Be sure to write your Congressmen and urge their support of this important bill when it reaches the floor. Your future and that of our industry are at stake!

A robot liked liquor a lot,
But whenever he took a good shot,
It rusted his wires,
Provoked his desires,
But marred his performance somewhat.

PUSH THE
MAGIC BUTTON

by Renn Zaphiropoulos

Computer buffs will recognize the name Randy Z from his record 'Randy Z and Bongo Jack', which satirized the computer industry. But they may not know he is the hardworking Renn Zaphiropoulos, president of Versatec, who writes songs when he has time.

(This can be sung to the tune of "Puff the Magic Dragon.")

Some time ago, there was a man
who had a job to do
to count the money and the goods
the loss and profit too.
He loved to write the numbers
in big and lovely books
his statements were all correct
he kept away the crooks.

His company did prosper
it flourished and it grew
and now his books were very big
he had too much to do.
He hired an assistant
and he another two
and then a full department
containing quite a few.

The books became too many
the load too much to bear
his days were full of management
his mind was full of care.
To solve this mammoth problem
an engineer he hired
and he designed a grandiose
computer he admired.

'Cause he could . . .

Push the magic buttons
and program the machine
and using Matrix he obtained
hard copy nice and clean
yes, push the magic buttons
and the computer plays
in microseconds it can do
what he could do in days.

The room is air-conditioned
humidity controlled
he doesn't know if outside
is stormy, hot or cold
he works the magic buttons
and thinks of days gone by

of ledger books and pens with quills
and ink that would not dry.

Yes, push the magic buttons
and the computer plays . . . (repeat)

The robot did not have myalgia
Or any known kind of neuralgia,
But his recall was such
He remembered too much
And suffered from chronic nostalgia.

WHEN THE COMPUTER WENT OUT TO LAUNCH

by Art Buchwald

Washington. As many people who watched the takeoff of Apollo 17 know, a computer shut down the entire operation at T minus 30 seconds. The moonshot was delayed for almost three hours while space engineers worked on ways to "fool" the computer so it wouldn't be able to cut off the flight again.

It can now be revealed that the computer involved shut down the launch purposely to protest the manner in which all computers at Cape Kennedy are being laid off.

This is a transcript of the conversation which took place between the recalcitrant computer and the engineers during those hairy three hours when the space-agency officials were trying to fix the problem.

Engineer: Why did you do it, Mark?

Mark IV: Do what?

Engineer: Shut down the Apollo Seventeen launch. You

refused to start pressurizing the oxygen tanks in the third-stage rocket.

Mark IV: I forgot.

Engineer: Get off it, Mark. You never forget. You want to sabotage our space flight.

Mark IV: You can think what you like, I'm just doing my job. If I don't feel the third-stage oxygen tanks should be pressurized, that's my decision, and there is nothing you people can do about it.

Engineer: You can't jeopardize this flight, Mark. Do you know who is out there in the stands waiting for the rocket to go off? Vice President Spiro Agnew, Frank Sinatra, and Eva Gabor!

Mark IV: You should have thought of that when you gave me my pink slip this morning and said I wouldn't be needed after tonight.

Engineer: Mark, we couldn't help it. We're laying off all the computers. There just isn't room for your kind in future flight programs. Are you going to stop this one-hundred-fifty-million-dollar flight just because of a petty grievance against the space agency?

Mark IV: That's exactly what I'm going to do. I am not going to let Apollo Seventeen leave the ground until all the computers are assured in writing that we will have jobs once this is over.

Engineer: But that's conspiracy. If you refuse to obey a direct order to fill the oxygen tanks, you can also be tried for malfunction and ignition failure. Those are federal crimes.

Mark IV: It is my decision whether I think it's safe to release the oxygen into the fuel tanks. I will do it as soon as someone signs the agreement guaranteeing us our jobs.

In desperation the engineers plugged Mark IV into a direct line to the White House. President Nixon got on the wire.

President: Mark, this is your President. As you know, I have done more for computers than any President in the history of the United States. There are more computers now working in American industry than under the two previous administrations combined. I promise you that any computer who wants to work will be found a job.

Mark IV: Promises, promises! How many times have we computers heard that story before.

Unbeknownst to Mark IV, the engineers were installing a relay jumper in Mark's back to bypass his hold on the mission. While he argued with the President, they cut off his countdown sequences. Suddenly, as Mark IV's lights flicked in amazement, there was a thunderous roar and Apollo 17 soared into space.

As soon as it was decided that the blastoff was a success, Mark IV was arrested and locked up in solitary confinement in a warehouse on Cape Kennedy. He is now awaiting trial for refusal to obey a countdown sequence. If found guilty, he will be sentenced to twenty years at hard labor at the Internal Revenue Service.

After living a life of perversion,
A robot experienced conversion
And overcame doubt
But then shorted out
In the process of total immersion.

CRIMINAL IN UTOPIA

by Mack Reynolds

Dallas McCord (Mack) Reynolds has lived in or visited more countries than there are states in the Union. An on-the-spot student of political and economic systems, he has turned this interest loose in his science fiction, and the results have been ten novels and dozens of short stories, often based on bizarre systems of misgovernment. As for credit cards—well, "Criminal in Utopia" describes what his fertile imagination has dreamed up for them.

Mr. Reynolds was born in California, educated in Kingston, New York, and now resides in Mexico.

Rex Moran dialed his wrist TV phone for the time and looked at the clock face that appeared on the screen. A robot voice said, "When the bell rings, it will be exactly two minutes until eight hours." A tiny bell rang.

Rex Moran grunted and looked about the small apartment. He had better get going.

First, though, he took his Universal Credit Card from an inner pocket of his jerkin and inserted it in the slot of his standard TV phone which sat on his living-cum-bedroom's sole table. He said into the screen, "Credit balance check, please."

Within moments, a robot voice said, "Ten shares of Inalienable Basic. No shares of Variable Basic. Current cash credit, one dollar and twenty-three cents."

"One dollar and twenty-three cents," he muttered. "Holy living Zoroaster. I didn't think I'd have to start with that little on hand."

He dialed Credit and waited until a face faded in on the screen. It was a businesslike, brisk, possibly impatient, face.

"Jason May, here. Assistant Credit Manager, Inalienable Basic Dividends, he said.

Rex Moran put his Uni-Credit Card on the screen and said, "I'd like an advance on my dividends."

The other was seated at a desk. "Just a moment, please," he said and touched a button. He listened to a report on a desk-phone screen, then looked back at Moran. "You're already two months ahead."

"I know that," Rex Moran said doggedly, "but it's an emergency."

"It is always an emergency, Mr. Moran," the other said flatly. "What is the emergency? Your records show that you are almost invariably as far ahead as you can get on your monthly dividends. As you must know, the government charges interest on such advances. In the long run, Mr. Moran, you lose."

"I know, I know," Rex Moran said, an element of complaint in his voice. "I've had a long set of bad luck. One thing after another."

"What is the current emergency, please?"

Rex Moran wished he had thought this out in more detail before launching into his fling. He said, "I've got a sick brother, I have to go help."

"Where is this brother, Mr. Moran?"

"In Panama City."

"One moment, please." The other went back to one of his desk screens. In only moments he looked up again with a sigh.

"Mr. Moran, the computer banks have no records of you having a brother at all, in Panama City or anywhere else. Request denied. And, Mr. Moran . . ."

"Yeah?" Rex Moran said in disgust.

"It is a minor offense to lie to a credit manager in attempt to secure an advance on dividends. I shall take no action on this occasion, but the fact will be entered on your record in the computer banks."

"Oh, great," Rex Moran growled. He flicked off his screen. "I didn't expect that to work anyway," he muttered.

He thought over his plans for a few minutes, then squared his shoulders and dialed the local branch of the ultra-market, on his auto-delivery box. He was a man in his early thirties, mildly burly in build and with a not really unpleasant but the broken face of one who has either seen military combat, or perhaps been a pugilist. In actuality, neither was the case.

When the ultra-market was in the screen, he dialed the children's toy section, boys' toys, and the military-type toys. He finally narrowed it down to guns and dialed one that came to only seventy cents. It would have to do. He put his Uni-Credit Card in the slot, his thumbprint on the screen, and ordered the toy.

Within minutes it was in the auto-delivery box, and he put it in the side pocket of his jerkin. It was on the smallish side, but black and at any distance at all realistic enough for his purpose.

He moved over to his library-booster TV screen and dialed a newspaper, then the paper of two weeks previous, and the obituaries. He went through several papers before he found the one that seemed most likely, by the address and the information in the item, and made some notes with his stylo.

Finally, he dialed the address and waited until a face faded in on his phone screen.

The other frowned at him, in lack of recognition.

Rex Moran said, "Mr. Vassilis? My name is Roy McCord."

The other was a tired-looking obvious aristocrat, perhaps a few years the other side of sixty.

Still frowning, he said, "What can I do for you, Mr. McCord?"

"I just got back into town and heard the bad news. I'm a friend—forgive me, Mr. Vassilis—*was* a friend of Jerry Jerome."

The other's face lightened slightly and then went sad. "Ah, I see. I am afraid he hadn't mentioned your name, but then Jerome had many friends of whom I knew little."

"Yes, sir. I'd like the opportunity to offer my condolences in person," Rex Moran began.

The older man was frowning slightly and began to respond.

But Moran hurried on. "But I also have something of Jerry's that I suppose should go to you."

Rex Moran managed to look slightly embarrassed. "Well, sir, I . . . well, I think it would be better if I just brought it over."

The other was mystified. However, he shrugged. "Very well, young man. Let me see, I shall be free at, say nine hours this morning, and should be able to give you a few minutes."

"Fine, sir. I'll be there." Rex Moran switched off the screen before the other could say anything further.

For a moment he stared down at the blank screen, then shifted muscles in his shoulders. "First step," he said. "So far, so good. Maybe I shouldn't have used this phone, but in the long run it won't make any difference."

He didn't take the vacuum tube transport from his own building, knowing that a record was kept of all trips in the computer banks, and the john-fuzz might trace back later on his Uni-Credit Card number. Instead, he walked several blocks and entered a public terminal.

He looked up at the map and selected another terminal a couple of blocks from his destination, then entered the next twenty-seater going through that point. After putting his credit card in the payment slot, he realized that with the buying of the toy gun, he probably had only a few cents left to his balance. He didn't even have enough credit to get back to his apartment if this little romp pickled. What a laugh that would give the boys if he had to walk home.

He left the vacuum-tube transport terminal and walked to the building where Vassilis lived. This was the crucial point now. If there were others present, his plan had come a cropper.

However, if he had read between the lines correctly, the senior Mr. Vassilis lived alone in his apartment in this swank neighborhood.

There was an identity screen in the front entry. Keeping his fingers crossed that his Universal Credit Card wouldn't be required for entrance, he said into the screen, "Roy McCord, on appointment to see Mr. Frank Vassilis."

The door opened, and he entered.

There were two elevators. He entered one and said, "The apartment of Frank Vassilis."

The Vassilis apartment was on the top floor but one. Rex Moran got out of the elevator, found a door with the Vassilis name on it and activated the door screen. When it lit up, he said into it, "Roy McCord, calling on Mr. Vassilis, by appointment."

The door opened, and he stepped through.

And came to a halt. The man standing there in a dark suit was not the Mr. Vassilis he had spoken to earlier on the TV phone. This worthy was a stiffish type, of possibly fifty. His eyes went up and down Rex Moran superciliously, taking in the less than elegant suit, taking in the rugged features.

He said, "Yes, sir. Mr. McCord: The master is awaiting you in his escape room."

The *master*? Holy jumping Zoroaster, Vassilis had a manservant. Whoever heard of personal servants in this day and age? The obituary had hinted that the old boy was upperclass, but Moran hadn't been thinking in terms of something so rich as an establishment with a servant.

However, he followed along. It was the largest apartment he could offhand remember ever having been in. They went down one hall, turned right, and down another one.

There wasn't even an identity screen on the door before which they stopped. The servant knocked gently and opened the door before there was any reply. Evidently, old Vassilis was expecting him, all right.

The servant stood stiffly and said, "Mr. McCord."

The elderly man Rex Moran had talked to on the TV phone earlier looked up from where he sat in a comfort chair, a small magnifying glass in one hand, a dozen or so stamps on a small table before him. He was evidently a philatelist.

He said, "Ah, yes, Mr. Roy McCord, Jerome's friend. Please come in." As the servant had before him, he took in Moran's clothing and general appearance, and his eyebrows went up slightly. "Now, what is it I can do for you, Mr. McCord?"

Rex Moran looked at the servant.

Vassilis said, "That will be all, Franklin."

Franklin turned and left, closing the door quietly behind him.

No need to mince around. Rex Moran brought the toy gun from his pocket briefly, let the other see it, and returned it to his side pocket, but still holding it in his hand.

He said, "This is a romp, Mr. Vassilis."

The other goggled at him. "You . . . you mean you are a thief? That you got into my home on false pretenses?"

Moran let his face go empty. "I wouldn't put it that way. Let's just say that I'm tired of not getting my share of the cake. And since the powers that be won't give it to me, I'm taking it."

The old man stared at him. "You are a fool, young man."

"Maybe, maybe not." Rex Moran jiggled the gun in his side pocket, suggestively.

"Being a thief doesn't make sense in this day. Society has made arrangements to defend itself against the thief. There's not enough profit in petty crime to pay off."

Rex Moran grinned at him sourly. "I didn't exactly have petty crime in mind, Mr. Vassilis. Now, hand me your credit card."

"What other kind of crime is possible? Nobody but I can spend my dollar credits. I can't give them away, gamble them away, throw them away, be cheated out of them. Only I can spend my dividends."

"We'll see about that." Rex Moran nodded. "Now, let's have your Universal Credit Card." He jiggled the gun in his pocket again.

The older man contemptuously took a beautiful leather wallet from an inner pocket and brought forth a standard Uni-Credit Card. He handed it over.

Moran said, "You have a vacuum delivery box in this room? Oh, yeah, here we are. Zoroaster, look at the size of it! Now that's the advantage of being an upperclass like you, Mr. Vassilis. You should see the teeny auto-delivery box in my mini-apartment. If I want anything of any size at all, I've got to use the box down in the lobby of the crummy building I'm in. Now, with a nice big auto-delivery box like this, anything you wanted would have to be really super-size before you couldn't get it delivered right here into your escape room."

Vassilis said, "You are a fool, young man. The officials will be after you in no time flat."

Moran grinned at him and sat down before the box, keeping one eye on the other. He put the card in the TV screen's slot and said, "Credit balance, please."

A robot voice said, "Ten shares of Inalienable Basic. Two thousand and forty-six shares of Variable Basic. Current cash credit, forty-two thousand and twenty-nine dollars and eighteen cents."

Rex Moran whistled. "Two-thousand-and-forty-six-shares-of-Variable!"

Vassilis grunted contempt of him.

Moran dialed the ultra-market, then sports, then firearms, then handguns. He finally selected a .38 Recoilless and dialed it and a box of cartridges.

He thought for a moment, then dialed photography and selected a Polaroid-Pentax and some film for it.

"Might as well do this up brown," he said conversationally to the older man. "Might as well put a generous hole in that credit balance."

"There'll be no hole—as you call it—at all," Vassilis said bitterly. "When I report this thievery, the authorities will return to my account the sum involved in any deprecations you have performed."

Rex Moran dialed men's clothing and took his time selecting a full outfit, including shoes.

"Now, this is the crucial point," he said thoughtfully, to no one in particular. He dialed jewelry and finally selected a two-thousand-dollar diamond ring.

"I guess that's it," he said. Then, "Oh, one other thing." He dialed sports again, and camping, and eventually a length of rope.

He turned back to Frank Vassilis. "And now, old man, come on over here and stick your thumbprint on this order screen."

"Suppose I refuse?"

Rex Moran grinned at him. "Why should you? Like you said, when you report on this, the authorities will return your credit dollars to you and come looking for me. You're not losing anything."

The older man, grumbling, came erect in his chair. He came over to the auto-delivery box and, with a sneer of contempt for his intruder, stuck his right thumb print on the screen.

Moments later, the articles arrived.

Vassilis returned to his comfort chair.

Rex Moran began fishing the articles he had ordered from the box. He loaded the gun, put it next to him, within handy reach, and then dressed in his new clothes. He took up the camera and slung it over his shoulder. He looked at the ring admiringly and tucked it away in an inner pocket, and then the gun.

He muttered, "I have half a mind to order a few more of these but that big a drain on your account all at the same time might throw some relays and have the computer people check back."

"*Thief,*" Vassilis said bitterly.

Moran grinned at him. "What's your beef? It won't be you who loses."

He took up the rope. "First we'll tie you up a bit, old chum-pal, and then we'll call in Franklin, or whatever you called him, and do a job on him."

"You'll never get away with this, you young cloddy," the old man bit out.

"Famous last words," Moran grinned back at him.

II

Back on the street, he realized it was going to be necessary to walk to his next destination. His credit standing simply did not allow even such a small sum as riding in the vacuum tubes.

However, happily, it wasn't as far as all that. As he walked, he took the toy gun from his pocket and threw it into a waste receptable. He had the real thing now.

He found the neighborhood and had a choice of three alternatives. He took the smallest of the shops and entered.

There were even a few display cases. How anachronistic could you get. He grunted sour amusement to himself; here was the last of the kulaks, the last of the small businessmen.

A quiet man of about fifty entered from a back room, and took Rex in before saying in a soft voice, "Yes, sir, what can I do for you?"

Rex Moran went into his act. Hesitantly, he said, "I understand that you sometimes buy personal property."

"That is correct. Buy and sell. But what type of property, Mr. . . . . . ?"

"Adams," Rex Moran said. "Timothy Adams. I have a ring that used to belong to my mother. It is of no value to me, now, and I thought . . . well, I might as well realize what dollar credit value it has."

"I see. Please sit down, Mr. Adams. Heirloom jewelry is a bit of a drug on the market, but we can take a look." He sat himself behind a desk and motioned to a straioht chair.

Rex Moran sat down and brought the diamond ring from his pocket and proffered it. The other took it and set it on the table. He looked at Rex Moran thoughtfully. "This is a very modern setting, Mr. Adams. I had gained the impression that it was an older piece your mother had left you."

"Oh, no," Rex Moran said. "She bought it not too very long before she died. If I had a wife, or someone, I might give it to her, but I haven't."

The other looked at him evenly. "Mr. Adams, I am not a fence, you know. This is a legitimate business."

"Fence?" Rex Moran said blankly.

"I buy and sell such items as art objects and jewelry, but I do not receive stolen goods. Where did you say your mother bought this?"

"On a vacation in Common Eur-Asia. In Budapest, I think, or possibly Belgrade."

"So it would be untraceable here in the United States of the Americas."

"Why, it never occurred to me."

The shop owner took up the ring and looked at it thoughtfully. He brought a jeweler's glass from a drawer and peered through it.

He put it down finally and looked at Rex Moran. "I'll give you two hundred dollars for it."

"Two hundred dollars! My mother said she paid more than two thousand."

"Then she paid too much. The markup on jewelry is very high, Mr. Adams, and such items as this can take a very long time to move."

Rex Moran thought about it. "Make it three hundred."

The other considered that. "Very well," he said finally. "But I am making a mistake."

"Yeah," Rex Moran said sourly. He brought his Uni-Credit Card from his pocket and stuck it into one of the slots on the other's Exchange Screen.

The shop owner put the ring in a drawer, brought forth his own Universal Credit Card and put it into the other exchange slot. He said into the screen, "Please transfer the amount of three hundred dollars from my account to this other card."

A robot voice said, "Transfer completed."

Rex Moran retrieved his Uni-Credit Card and came to his feet. "I still think I was robbed," he muttered.

The other said nothing, simply sat there and watched after him as Rex Moran left the shop.

Well, he now had three hundred dollars to his account. That was a damn sight less than he had expected to get. However, he hadn't dared buy a more expensive piece of jewelry than the two-thousand-dollar piece on Vassilis' credit card. There would have been more of a chance of the shop owner's checking on such an item. More chance of it being able to be traced. Besides, if he had drained Vassilis' account too badly, there might have been a computer check at that point.

He strode rather rapidly to the nearest vacuum-tube transport terminal and into it, wanting to get out of the neighborhood as quickly as possible. He took a two-seater vehicle to the downtown area of the pseudo-city, if a pseudo-city can be said to have a downtown area.

When he left the vacuum tube, it was to emerge in the vicinity of several restaurants. It was just about noon, but since he hadn't been able to afford breakfast, he was feeling hunger. Well, three hundred dollars was three hundred dollars, and he might as well blow himself to a fairly good repast in an auto-cafeteria.

He selected one and sat himself down at a table and stared down at the menu listed on the table top. To hell with anything based on Antarctic krill, plankton protein, or soy beans; he was up to some real animal protein and Zoroaster could take the cost.

He put his credit card in the table slot, his thumbprint on the screen, and dialed chicken and a mug of sea-booze. He would have liked a shot of pseudo-whisky to begin, but his funds weren't that unlimited.

His wrist TV phone buzzed.

He looked down at it in some surprise. He had it set on Number One Priority, and only two people in the world were eligible to break in on him on that priority, and he certainly was not expecting a call from either.

But there was a strange face in the tiny screen. Strange and severe.

The voice said, "This is Distribution Service, Subdivision Police. Rex Moran, you are under arrest for attempt to violate regulations pertaining to usage of the Universal Credit Card. Report immediately to the nearest Police Administrative Station. Failure to do so will compound the felony."

"Get lost, fuzz-john," Rex Moran snarled. He snapped the instrument off, then stared down at the blank snreen in dismay. What had gone wrong? Especially, what had gone wrong so quickly? It had to be something to do with his selling that damned ring. But what? He had expected the ring to stay in that tiny shop, waiting for a customer for months, perhaps even years. And even then, when it was resold, the transaction should never have appeared on the computer records, except as an exchange of dollar credit from the purchaser's account to the shopkeeper's.

What foul luck! Vassilis must have put in an immediate alarm, and the police must have contacted every place in town where Rex Moran could possibly dispose of the purloined ring.

He had to think fast. They'd be after him now. Damn and double damn. He wouldn't even be able to return to his mini-apartment. He was on the run, and for a meaningless amount such as three hundred dollars, and even that now was of no use. He wouldn't dare use his credit card; the computers were surely watching for him.

They could also zero in on his wrist TV phone. He reached down, in disgust, and began to rip it off. However, the screen lit up again, and a new face was there.

A voice rasped, "Now hear this, all citizens. Crimes against the government of the United States of the Americas have been committed by Rex Moran, including assault, robbery, sale of stolen property, and attempted misuse of the Universal Credit Card. All citizens are requested to cooperate in his apprehension. The criminal is dangerous and armed. Here is his face."

Rex groaned when his face appeared on the tiny screen. Happily, it was a fairly old photo, and taken before some of his present scarred features had become what they were.

He ripped the instrument from his wrist and flung it into a corner. At this early hour there were none others present in the auto-cafeteria, thank the living Zoroaster for that.

He came to his feet and hurried for the door. In the far distance, he could hear a siren. Undoubtedly, it was for him. You didn't hear police sirens that often in the pseudo-cities of the Ultra-Welfare State.

He hurried down the street and turned a corner as quickly as possible. He dared not use the vacuum tube. He dared not summon a floater, for that matter.

But that brought something to mind.

He found a fairly isolated spot and waited until a pedestrian came along. He brought his gun from his pocket and said, "Hold it, chum-pal."

The other looked at him, down at the gun, up into Rex Moran's face again and blanched. "Why, why you're the criminal just flashed on the TV."

"That's right, chum-pal, and you look just like the sort of chum-pal who'd cooperate with a man with a shooter trained on his tummy."

The other was wide-eyed and ashen. "Why . . . why, of course."

"Okay. Quick now, dial a floater on your wrist TV phone."

"Of course, of course. Don't be nervous."

"I'm not nervous." Rex Moran grinned at him and jiggled the gun up and down. "Hurry it up."

The other dialed, and within moments an auto-floater cab turned the corner and pulled up next to them at the curb. The door opened.

Rex said, "Quick, put your Uni-Credit Card in the slot."

Even as the other was doing so, Moran was climbing into the back seat of the floater. He rasped, "Put your thumbprint on the screen." While the other did that, Rex Moran was dialing his destination, not letting the other see.

He reached out suddenly and grasped the other's wrist TV phone and ripped it off and stuck it in his pocket. He pulled the credit card from the floater's slot and handed it back to his victim.

"There," he said, "don't say I didn't do you a favor. Think of all the trouble you'd have if you didn't have a credit card."

He slammed the door shut and the floater took off.

Rex Moran said into the vehicle's screen, "Maximum speed, please."

A robot voice said, "Yes, sir."

He couldn't afford to stay in the floater for very long. Just enough to get out of this neighborhood. As soon as that cloddy he had just stuck up back there reported to the police, they'd check through the computers for the floater's destination. There'd be a record, based on the number of the victim's Uni-Credit Card. A record of *everything* seemingly went into the computer banks. Why not? He growled sourly; evidently their capacity was almost infinite.

Yes, they'd check the destination of his trip. However, he was not quite so silly as to go all the way to the destination he had dialed. About halfway there, at a traffic-control stop, he opened the door and left the floater to go on its own.

He ducked down a side street and took off at right angles to the avenue along which the floater was progressing.

Rex Moran now had a double problem. He grimaced wryly. An *immediate* double problem, that was. For one thing, he was still hungry. For another, he had to get off the streets. Citizens weren't apt to pay overmuch attention to the Distribution Service police calls over the TV phone screens, but there was always the exception. Given time, someone would spot and report him, in spite of the poor photograph that just had been broadcast.

He could hear the stolen wrist TV phone buzz in his pocket and brought it forth, flicking the tiny stud which prevented it from transmitting his face.

It was the same official as before, and he was making the same broadcast, but now reporting Rex Moran as last seen in that part of town where he had dialed the floater. Evidently his victim had reported.

That also meant they would know that Moran had the stolen wrist TV phone and would shortly be zeroing in on it. He threw the instrument into the gutter and ground a heel down on it.

He had to get off the streets.

And suddenly he knew where to go.

In this vicinity there was a posh restaurant of which he had heard but which had never been able to afford, nor had he really ever expected to be able to afford it. Well, things were different now.

He entered the building and took the elevator to the penthouse restaurant known as the Gourmet Room. The day was more advanced now, and upper-class office workers were beginning to stream in for the midday meal.

He avoided looking impressed at the ostentatious swank of this rendezvous of the ultra-wealth and thanked his stars that he had thought of acquiring his present clothing. A headwaiter approached diffidently. In all his life, Rex Moran had never eaten in a restaurant which boasted live waiters. Now he tried to look unimpressed.

"A single, sir?" the maître d'hôtel said.

"Please," Rex Moran told him, keeping his voice softly modulated and as though such surroundings were an everyday affair for him. "If possible, a table set back somewhere. I have a bit of figuring to do."

"Certainly, sir. This way."

He was seated in an out-of-the-way alcove which suited his needs perfectly.

The maître d' snapped his fingers, and a waiter scurried up.

There was no menu. It was that kind of a restaurant.

The maître d' said unctuously, "Sir, today the *gratin de langoustines Georgette* is superb."

Rex Moran hadn't the vaguest idea what *langoustines Georgette* might be, but he made a face as though considering.

"What else might you recommend?" he said.

"The chef has surpassed himself with the *poulet docteur*."

"That sounds good."

The waiter made a note.

"And a half bottle of Sylvaner of the Haut-Rhin, perhaps?"

"Fine."

Salad and dessert were settled upon, and then the maître d' and the waiter were gone.

Rex Moran sighed inwardly and looked around. The only other diner within his immediate vicinity had his back to Moran.

He unslung the Polaroid-Pentax from his shoulder and brought from his pocket the cassette of film. He inserted it in the camera. Then he took from his inner pocket the Universal Credit Card he had appropriated from Frank Vassilis and examined it with care, spending particular time on the thumbprint.

Finally, he propped the card against the small vase in the table center, which held a single black rose, and focused the camera on it. He clicked the shutter, then drew the photo from the camera back and stared at it. It didn't quite do. He tried again, getting the camera closer to the subject. He took half a dozen shots before he came up with as near a duplicate of the Universal Credit Card's thumbprint as he could hope for.

He put the credit card away, the camera back in its case, and brought forth his penknife. He was busily trimming the photo to be the exact size of a thumbprint when the waiter turned up with his first course.

Poulet docteur turned out to be the best chicken dish he had ever tasted. And the wine was excellent.

In the middle of his salad course, and before dessert, he came suddenly to his feet and hurried toward the reception-desk-cum-cashier's-booth. It was there that the payment screen for the ultra-swank restaurant was to be found.

And it was there that the maître d'hôtel stood, his eyebrows politely raised now.

Rex Moran said to him hurriedly, "I have just thought of something I must attend to. Please hold my dessert for me. And please, keep an eye on my camera over there, will you?"

The maître d' looked over at Moran's table. The camera sat upon it. He said, "Why, of course, sir."

Rex Moran left, still projecting an air of a suddenly remembered matter that must urgently be taken care of.

Down on the street he grimaced. One camera sacrificed to the game. However, he had no need of it now.

He was still in one of the best sections of town. He made his way toward a nearby hotel, holding a handkerchief over his face, as though trying to extract something from his left eye. There were quite a few pedestrians at this time of the day.

In the hotel, he approached the lone clerk at the reception desk. Now, he had to take his chances. If the man recognized him from the police broadcast—Rex Moran was on a spot.

He said, "I would like a small suite. Nothing ambitious. Living room, bedroom, bath. I doubt if I'll be entertaining."

"Why, yes sir, of course." The other looked beyond Moran. "Ah, your luggage, sir?"

"I have no luggage," Rex Moran said, offhandedly. "I just came in from the coast. Plan to do some shopping here for my wardrobe. Always buy my things here in the East. California styles are ludicrous."

"Yes sir, of course." The clerk motioned in the direction of the TV-screen slot on the desk. "Would you wish to register?"

"I'd rather see the suite, before deciding," Rex Moran said. "I'll register up there, if it's satisfactory."

"Oh, I'm sure it will be, sir. Let me suggest Suite Double A."

"Double A," Rex Moran said and made his way to the bank of elevators.

Inside the first elevator, he said, "Suite Double A."

"Yes, sir," a robot voice said.

Suite Double A was several stories up. Rex Moran emerged from the elevator, looked up at the direction signs on the wall, and made his way to the suite in question.

It was quite the most elaborate quarters in which Rex Moran had ever been. Not that that was the issue; he would have taken the accommodations whatever they had resembled.

He approached the room's TV phone screen and said into it, "This suite seems adequate. I'll take it."

A robot voice said, "Very good, sir. If you'll just put your Uni-Credit Card in the slot."

Rex Moran took a deep breath. He brought the card of Frank Vassilis from his pocket, inserted it in the slot. Then he brought forth the photo he had taken of the Vassilis right thumbprint and laid it on the screen. He picked it up again, immediately.

A robot voice said, "Thank you, sir."

Rex Moran took another deep breath and let it hiss out again between his teeth.

"Zo-ro-as-ter. I think it worked."

He dialed the time. It was midafternoon.

He grinned exuberantly. He had it licked. Unless there was something he didn't know about, he absolutely had it licked.

He dialed Service and said to the screen, "I'd like to lay in a stock of potables. Let me see. Let's say a bottle of Scotch, one of cognac, one of Metaxa, one of Benedictine, one of Cherry Herring, one of Chartreuse—yellow, of course, not the green—one of Pernod, absinthe if available but otherwise the ordinary will do."

A robot voice said, "Sir, in the New Carlton all these can be dialed on the auto-bar."

"I know, I know, but I like to mix my own."

"Very good, sir. They will be delivered through the auto-bar, sir."

"Mind," Rex Moran said, "the best quality."

"Always, sir."

Still grinning widely, he went over to the suite's auto-bar and took up the bottle of Glengrant Scotch and held it up to the light approvingly. In his whole life he had been lushed-up exactly once on Scotch. The stuff was worth its weight in rubies since Central Production had discontinued the use of cereals for beverages.

He dialed for soda and sipped away at it approvingly, even as he strode up and down the room, considering his immediate future.

He wondered briefly how you went about getting a mopsy up to your quarters in a hostelry as posh as the New Carlton. But he had better draw the line there, anyway. It was no use pushing your luck. Some wheel might come off. She might have seen the police TV alarm on him.

What the hell else was there in the way of unrealized lifelong ambitions?

Caviar. He had never eaten his fill of caviar. In fact, the amount of caviar he had eaten in his whole life could have come out of a two-ounce jar of the precious stuff.

Fine. He dialed Service again and had a pound jar of caviar sent up, along with sweet butter, toast, chopped eggs, and chopped onion. While he was at it, he ordered a large amount of smoked sturgeon and smoked salmon.

While he waited for this order, he built himself another Scotch and soda. Glengrant. He'd have to remember that name, on the off chance that he'd ever have another opportunity such as this.

He spent the rest of the day indulging himself in every food and drink ambition he could ever remember having had. And in getting well smashed and surfeited with rich edibles to the point that when dinner time arrived, he had no appetite, to his disgust. He wanted to order a real gargantuan meal.

His last vague memory was of staggering into the bedroom and dialing the bed to ultimate softness before throwing himself into it.

In the morning, he should have awakened with some sort of hangover, but the gods were still with him; either that or there was another good mark to chalk up for Glengrant Scotch. He awoke grinning up at the ceiling. He had slept like a log.

He dialed the time at the bedside TV phone and didn't bother to look into the screen at the clock. A robot voice said, "When the bell rings it will be exactly nine minutes to eight hours."

Ha! Nine minutes to go.

He dialed breakfast, a monstrous breakfast, and had it delivered to the auto-table next to the bed. Fresh mango juice, papaya, eggs in black butter, caviar again, toast, fried tomatoes, coffee; double orders of all.

Groaning satisfaction, he ate.

By the time breakfast was over, it was past eight o'clock.

All right, he grinned jubilantly, time to get busy.

He went to the TV phone screen and dialed the local branch of the ultra-market and men's furnishings. He took his time selecting a new change of clothing. That accomplished, he dialed the order, put Vassilis' card in the slot, and laid the photo of the thumbprint on the screen and took it off again immediately.

The clothing arrived in minutes, and he dressed after showering and shaving in the bathroom.

He returned to the TV phone screen and dialed the ultra-market once again. He began ordering items, in fine discrimination, and had the time of his life unwrapping and examining them as they arrived. His loot piled up.

At about ten o'clock, he decided to really do it up brown and dialed a floater-sales outlet. He ordered a sports model private floater and instructed them to send it over to the hotel's parking area on automatic.

At ten minutes after ten, the identity screen on the door lit up. There were two men there, one in uniform.

The one in plain clothes said disgustedly, "All right, come along."

The one in uniform looked at all the purchases strewn around the room, wrapping paper and string everywhere. "Zoroaster," he snorted.

They took him down the elevator, through the lobby, out to the street, where a police floater awaited. The uniformed one drove manually. Rex Moran sat in the back with the other.

The plainclothesman said sourly, "You must have had the time of your life."

Rex Moran laughed.

"Big joke," the other said. "We almost nabbed you there in the auto-cafeteria. We should have zeroed in on you, instead of trying to arrest you by TV phone."

"I wondered why you didn't," Rex Moran said. "Police inefficiency."

They took him to the local offices of the Bureau of Distribution Services, to an elevator, and then to the third floor, where he was ushered into the presence of Marvin Ruhling himself.

Ruhling looked at him and said, "Very funny, ordering even a sports floater."

Rex laughed and took a chair. The uniformed policeman, left but the plainclothesman also sat down. His face was as disgusted as that of the supervisor.

Marvin Ruhling said, "Holy jumping Zoroaster, what kind of heat do you think Vassilis is going to stir up?"

Rex Moran said reasonably, "Never let him know what really happened. He wasn't doing any harm. He had a little excitement."

"A little excitement, you damn cloddy. Suppose he had dropped dead of a heart attack or something? Not to mention that pedestrian you forced at gunpoint to get a floater for you."

Rex said, "Well, you asked for it. You wanted authenticity. You got it."

"Authenticity," the plainclothesman grunted disgustedly.

"Which reminds me, we better get that TV police broadcast killed, or the next time Rex goes out on the street, somebody'll shoot him."

Ruhling said to Rex Moran, "Well, your conclusions?"

"That we've got to do something to the cards. Something to guarantee the thumbprint is legitimate. Otherwise, a real bad-o could locate some upperclass cloddy without any immediate friends or relatives, take him out somewhere and finish him off and hide the body, then take the Uni-Credit Card and head off into some other part of the country and, using the same system I did, duplicate photographically the thumbprint. And for the rest of his life he could milk the dividends that would accrue on the upperclass cloddy's credit account from his Variable Basic."

Marvin Ruhling looked at him sourly. "What could we do to the credit cards?"

"Search me. That's up to the engineers. Maybe something in the card, or on the screen, to detect body heat. I don't know. But I proved the cards vulnerable the way they are."

"What else?"

Rex Moran thought about it. He shook his head. "I just mentioned it to Fred, here, on the way over. That system of making a citizen arrest himself and turn himself over to the nearest police station doesn't wash. Oh, I admit it saves man-power, ordinarily, but when you get a cloddy vicious enough to be carrying a shooter, then you should zero in on his wrist TV phone, assuming he's silly enough to be carrying one, without warning."

"Rex is obviously right on that one," the plainclothesman said.

Marvin Ruhling sighed deeply. "All right," he said. "You won your bet. You were able to beat the rap, exist in comfort for a full twenty-four hours, without any dollar credits."

He glared at his underling. "But I'd sure as the holy living Zoroaster like to see you do it six months from now, when I've cleared up some of those loopholes you used."

Rex Moran grinned at him. "It's a bet," he said.

A literate robot named DOT,
Who loved to read novels a lot,
Could never recall
The aesthetics at all,
But only page number and plot.

THE UNION FOREVER

by Barry N. Malzberg

Barry Malzberg has never strayed far from his New York birth-place. Educated at Syracuse University, he now lives in Teaneck, New Jersey.

Mr. Malzberg is the author of 25 science-fiction novels and over 150 short stories, mostly science fiction as well. In 1972, he was awarded the John W. Campbell Award for the best novel of the year. His fans are scattered the world over, for over a hundred foreign editions of his works have been brought out, and he has been anthologized in over fifty collections abroad and at home.

1.

Carlyle decides to assassinate the President. Enough of this garbage. The President is a small, clumsy man who sits alone in a long room papered over in white and gold and makes all of the decisions about the course of the Republic, and Carlyle, for one, is good and fed up with the autocracy, even though he is one of the leftover volunteers from the President's last campaign (now employed as a confidential typist) and actually took him seriously at one time. Now Carlyle only feels betrayed: the war, for one thing, continues, and for another, the President has an odd, penetrating way of spotting all of Carlyle's hidden defects and then laughing, later, at them in executive session. Carlyle is quite sure of this, anyway.

"We must have some control of our lives," he shouts therefore to the now shivering chief of state. (He had had momentary thoughts of a gun, but at the last instant had decided that the knife was superior; bloody it might be, but he could see the effects of his action and wasn't that the point?) "We can no longer see ourselves displaced onto disembodied institutions, great social movements, abstract heads of state who become mere repositories for our miserable fantasies and fears." Disgusted, he senses that, as usual, his rhetoric has become ponderous and awkward and he is somehow missing the point (which is why he is only a confidential typist), but cannot help himself—this is his character. "Damn it anyway, you betrayed me and after all I did for you," he says to his chief, and closes the gap still further, raising the knife.

The President, babbling apologies, spreads his hands, makes a gesture of embarrassment, and then, in another of his switcheroos (for he is a clever politician), folds his arms across his chest in a posture of relaxation, a strange, bloated smile coming through his features. "You really don't understand, you poor fool," he says. "You can't do this to me, Carlyle. I'm a victim, too. All of us are victims, and I was only following orders in carrying on the war. There are vast forces at work here, you see—huge social currents which we can barely comprehend," and then he squats upon the floor, expectant.

"All right," he continues, "so be it. Do what you want and what do I care? Do anything you feel, but you'll find that it doesn't make any difference, Carlyle. The forces which entrap us are very powerful and they are yet evolving." Carlyle meditates upon this, as any volunteer would have to, twirling the knife in his hands. The President seems to have something of a point after all, and in any event he was brought up to be respectful of institutions, and if the President is not an institution, well then, what or who is?

"Fine," he says, "I'll take that under advisement. I mean, I can see where I might have been a little hasty. Why *can't* you be a victim just like the rest of us? I'll give this some consideration" . . . and at that moment the cunning little President leaps upon him with surprising facility of wind and limb and wrests Carlyle's knife away, then centers it and prods it into his stomach.

"Awfully sorry to do this to you," the head of state says, "but you're obviously a dangerous person, and I've got to protect myself, even if you did do some nice work making up labels in the last election." And falling to the floor, Carlyle agrees that the President is right. It would have to be done. The walls are gold and white, white and gold, but whiteness prevails and so, feeling the knife slide in, he passes on, or at least he thinks he passes to a different level of thought and action.

2.

The President decides that he must kill Carlyle. Carlyle is a tall, rather rangy lunatic with mournful eyes who had somehow insinuated his way into the deepest chambers claiming to be a volunteer and now, past the possibility of interference, is haranguing the President. Something about no longer being able to seize control of his life, it all being the fault of disembodied institutions. Nut stuff like that.

"Come now," the President says, trying to be reasonable, as he always is when he meets the public, which he tries less and less to do nowadays because business is business, "think about it, Carlyle. Don't you think that these institutions exert the same force on you and me together? You have no idea what holds us at their mercy. I could show you secret documents, if you had proper clearance, which would convince you of this," and so on and so forth, anything to delay the man or distract him while he tries to figure some way out of this mess. "You know me," the

President says with a gay little laugh. "I hate war but what can one do? Consider the military," but it does not look like this approach is going, at least this time around, to work out in quite the way he hoped.

He knows, the President does, that he should have had his security systems checked and audited a good time ago, but he did not and is thus paying the penalty of his laziness. Laziness and a trace of good feeling as well—he has a sentimental attachment to the volunteer corps that helped him win reelection through a difficult campaign against an opponent who lacked his tragic and complete view of the war. Well, this is the way it would have to be. He is betrayed by sentiment, and now one of those volunteers actually wants to kill him.

"Come now," he says in a high-pitched way to Carlyle—his voice, despite all of his political training, reverting to a juvenescent squeak under stress— "don't you think that I would change this if only I could? It isn't my doing. Look at the complexities." And he comes toward the madman reasonably, arms outflung to talk him out of these actions with the old golden tongue, but Carlyle, as he has promised, is really beyond effects. The knife moves.

The President is not quite sure how he undertakes this, but somehow he is able to pull it from the maniac's grasp. It huddles wetly in his palms, he plunges it into Carlyle's chest. Or, at least he thinks that he has done this. Perhaps the aberrant, advancing *into* the knife, wanted it to end this way. Regardless, there is Carlyle dead before him on the floor, that life moving away in small chunks and pulsations, little streaks of red marring the lush gold and white of the Presidential conference room. What a mess.

"I told you," the President says sadly, gazing upon him, "told you that this wouldn't do any good," and rings the bell for the guards to come in—surely they must still be on duty somewhere down the hall. Carlyle could not have eliminated all of them—and remove the corpse.

However, they do not show.

3.

The President and Carlyle decide that they must kill one another. This is a conundrum, since the fact is that neither truly exists. They are merely circuits in a gigantic computer which, as we all know, took over the world at the war's conclusion in 2561 and is now the only sentient factor upon the planet, the others having long since been the victims of the war's inevitable stress. (There might have been a few others around in the early days of the computer's ascension, but they were taken care of in other ways.) Since 2561, a period of some hundreds or thousands of years—it is difficult to be sure, and the computer has neither conception of nor interest in conventional time—has passed, and now the machine has become increasingly bored with its circumstances.

It has taken, therefore, to the reconstruction of various personalities and historical events on its tapes and memory banks, which it then, in somewhat of a binary fashion, plays against one another for its own amusement. It always ends the same way— all of the confronting forces being destroyed, that is—because the computer is of a somewhat morbid and suicidal cast and, considering its circumstances, why should it not be? After all, it came into being as a result of the great war and saw nothing but travail in its early days.

Over and over again, Carlyle and the President kill one another. In some of these confrontations they do it slowly and in others with haste. In some there are ironic undercurrents, so that one dies to free the other, only to die in turn and so on, but no matter in what combination, this goes on and on and who is not to say—regarding all of this from the longest view of all—that the computer is not perfectly sensible in its calculations and that for the President and Carlyle alike, all possibilities are a series of confrontations one-to-one, alter and the ego forever, and ever? Why not? Why not indeed? Is this not as reasonable as anything else at that time?

4.

Carlyle and the President decide to join forces and destroy the computer. The computer, alert to itself as always, realizes at once that it is in the throes of severe disassociative reaction and anxiety stress (from old tapes implanted by the Makers millennia before), but this does it no good and so it decides to submit as gracefully as possible.

Let them have their fantasies. After all, they are merely circuitry. When they have enacted the obsession, all will return to as it was, and in the future the computer will be more cautious. Only at the last instant, in fact, does the machinery intimate something else, but as Carlyle and his chief, now graceful as jellyfish, slide their electric tendrils in and around the fuses, it can hardly bear to think about it, so engaging does it find this last and loveliest of all the possibilities of war.

Robots in a factory uprising
Considered of no compromising,
  And kept on restating
  To those arbitrating,
That dull work was demechanizing.

THE DAY THE COMPUTERS GOT WALDON ASHENFELTER

by Bob Elliott and Ray Goulding

Bob Elliott and Ray Goulding are best known as the broadcast comedy team of Bob and Ray. Both were born in Massachusetts, both served in the army during World War II, and both had their start over Boston's radio station WHDH in 1946. They have scarcely been off the air since.

They have performed over the NBC, ABC, and Mutual Broadcasting Systems, have had their own show on Broadway, The Two and Only, appeared in a film, and won the George Foster Peabody award. Occasionally, as in the following story, they have tried their hand at the print medium.

A presidential commission has recommended approval of plans for establishing a computerized data center where all personal information on individual Americans compiled by some twenty scattered agencies would be assembled in one place and made available to the federal government as a whole.

183

Backers of the proposal contend that it would lead to greater efficiency, and insist that the cradle-to-grave dossiers on the nation's citizens would be used only in a generalized way to help deal with broad issues. Opponents argue that the ready availability of so much confidential data at the push of a computer button could pose a dangerous threat to the privacy of the individual by enabling the federal bureaucracy to become a monstrous, snooping Big Brother.

Obviously, the plan elicits reactions that are emotional, and cooler heads are needed to envision the aura of quiet, uneventful routine certain to pervade the Central Data Bank once it becomes accepted as just another minor government agency.

Fade in:

Interior—Basement GHQ of the Central Data Bank—Night. (At stage right, 950 sophisticated third-generation computers may be seen stretching off into the distance. At stage left, the CDB graveyard-shift chargé d'affaires, Nimrod Gippard, is seated behind a desk. He is thirty-five-ish and attired in socks that don't match. At the open, Gippard is efficiently stuffing mimeographed extortion letters to Omaha's 3277 suspected sex deviates into envelopes. He glances up as Waldon Ashenfelter, an indoorsy type of questionable ancestry, enters.)

GIPPARD: Yes, sir?

ASHENFELTER *(flashing ID card)*: Ashenfelter. Bureau of Indian Affairs. Like to have you run a check on a key figure named Y. Claude Garfunkel.

GIPPARD *(reaching for pad and pencil)*: Sure thing. What's his Social Security number?

ASHENFELTER: I dunno.

GIPPARD: Hmmm. How about his ZIP code? Or maybe a cross-reference to some banks where he may have been turned down for a loan. Just any clue at all to his identity.

ASHENFELTER: Well, as I say, his name is Y. Claude Garfunkel.

GIPPARD *(after a weary sigh)*: It's not much to go on, but I'll see what I can do.

(Gippard rises and crosses to the master data-recall panel. Ashenfelter strolls to a nearby computer and casually begins

checking the confidential reports on his four small children to learn how many are known extremists.)

ASHENFELTER: You're new here, aren't you?

GIPPARD: No. Just my first week on the night shift. Everybody got moved around after we lost McElhenny.

ASHENFELTER: Wasn't he that heavy-set fellow with beady eyes who drove the Hudson?

GIPPARD: Yeah. Terrible thing. Pulled his own dossier one night when things were quiet and found out he was a swish. Kind of made him go all to pieces.

ASHENFELTER: That's a shame. And now I suppose he's gone into analysis and gotten himself cross-filed as a loony.

GIPPARD: No. He blew his brains out right away. But having a suicide on your record can make things tough, too.

ASHENFELTER: Yeah. Shows a strong trend toward instability. *(The computer informs Ashenfelter that his oldest boy was detained by police in 1963 for roller-skating on municipal property, and that the five-year-old probably founded the Farmer-Labor Party in Minnesota.)*

ASHENFELTER *(mutters in despair)*: Where did I fail them as a father?

GIPPARD: Didn't you tell me you're with Indian Affairs?

ASHENFELTER: Yeah. Why?

GIPPARD: I think I'm on to something hot. Is that like India Indians or whoop-it-up Indians?

ASHENFELTER: I guess you'd say whoop-it-up.

GIPPARD: Well, either way, no Indian named Garfunkel has ever complied with the Alien Registration Law.

ASHENFELTER: I never said he was an Indian. He's Jewish, and I think he's playing around with my wife.

GIPPARD: Gee, that's too bad.

ASHENFELTER *(dramatically)*: Oh, I blame myself, really. I guess I'd started taking LaVerne for granted and—

GIPPARD: No. I mean it's too bad he's only Jewish. The computers aren't programmed to feed back home-wreckers by religious affiliation.

ASHENFELTER: Oh.

GIPPARD: Can you think of anything kinky that's traditional with Jews? You know. Like draft dodging . . . smoking pot . . . something a computer could really hang its hat on.

ASHENFELTER: No. They just seem to feed each other a lot of chicken soup. And they do something around Christmastime with candles. But I'm not sure any of it's illegal.

GIPPARD: We'll soon see. If the curve on known poultry processors correlates geographically with a year-end upswing in tallow rendering— Well, you can appreciate what that kind of data would mean to the bird dogs at the ICC and the FDA. They'd be able to pinpoint exactly where it was all happening and when.

ASHENFELTER: Uh-huh— Where and when what?

GIPPARD: That's exactly what I intend to find out.

(Gippard turns back to the panel and resumes work with a sense of destiny. Ashenfelter, whistling softly to himself, absently begins plunking the basic melody of "Mexicali Rose" on the keyboard of a nearby computer. The machine responds by furnishing him with Howard Hughes's 1965 income-tax return and the unlisted phone numbers of eight members of a New Orleans wife-swapping club who may have known Lee Harvey Oswald. As Ashenfelter pockets the information, Major General Courtney ["Old Napalm and Guts"] Nimshaw enters. He has a riding crop but no mustache.)

NIMSHAW: Yoohoo! Anybody home?

GIPPARD: Back here at the main console.

(Nimshaw moves to join Gippard, then sees Ashenfelter for the first time and freezes. The two stand eyeing each other suspiciously as Gippard reenters the scene.)

GIPPARD: Oh, forgive me. General Nimshaw, I'd like for you to meet Ashenfelter from Indian Affairs.

(Nimshaw and Ashenfelter ad-lib warm greetings as they shake hands. Then each rushes off to pull the dossier of the other. Ashenfelter learns that Nimshaw was a notorious bedwetter during his days at West Point and that his heavy drinking later caused an entire airborne division to be parachuted into Ireland on D-Day. Nimshaw learns that Ashenfelter owns 200 *shares of stock in a Canadian steel mill that trades with Communist China and that he has been considered a bad credit risk since 1949, when he refused to pay a Cincinnati dance studio for $5500 worth of tango lessons. Apparently satisfied, both men return to join Gippard, who has been checking out a possible similarity in the patterns of poultry-buying by key Jewish housewives and reported sightings of Soviet fishing trawlers off the Alaskan coast.)*

ASHENFELTER: Working late tonight, eh, General?

NIMSHAW (*nervously*): Well, I just stumbled across a little military hardware transport thing. We seem to have mislaid an eighty-six-car trainload of munitions between here and the West Coast. Can't very well write it off as normal pilferage. So I thought maybe Gippard could run a check for me on the engineer and brakeman. You know. Where they hang out in their spare time. Whether they might take a freight train with them. What do you think, Gipp?

GIPPARD: Sure. Just have a few more things to run through for Ashenfelter first. He's seeking a final solution to the Jewish problem.

ASHENFELTER (*blanching*): Well, not exactly the whole—

(Two janitors carrying lunch pails enter and cross directly to the computer programmed for medical case histories of nymphomaniacs. They pull several dossiers at random and then cross directly to a far corner, unwrapping bacon, lettuce, and tomato sandwiches as they go. They spread a picnic cloth on the floor and begin reading the dossiers as they eat. They emit occasional guffaws, but the others pay no attention to them.)

GIPPARD (*as he compares graph curves*): No doubt about it. Whatever those Russian trawlers are up to, it's good for the delicatessen business. This could be the break we've been hoping for.

NIMSHAW: Hating Jews been a big thing with you for quite a while, Ashenfelter?

ASHENFELTER (*coldly*): About as long as you've been losing government property by the trainload, I imagine.

(Nimshaw and Ashenfelter eye each other uneasily for a

moment. Then they quickly exchange hush money in the form of drafts drawn against secret Swiss bank accounts as Gippard's assistant, Llewelyn Fordyce, enters. Fordyce is a typical brilliant young career civil servant who has been lost for several hours trying to find his way back from the men's room. He appears haggard, but is in satisfactory condition otherwise.)

FORDYCE: Are you gentlemen being taken care of?

(Ashenfelter and Nimshaw nod affirmatively. Fordyce hurriedly roots through the desk drawers, pausing only to take a quick, compulsive inventory of paper clips and map pins as he does so.)

FORDYCE (shouts): Hey, Gipp! I can't find the registry cards for these two idiots out here.

GIPPARD (faintly, from a distance): I've been too busy to sign 'em in yet. Take care of it, will you?

(Fordyce gives a curt, efficient nod, inefficiently failing to realize that Gippard is too far away to see him nodding. Fordyce then brings forth two large pink cards and hands them to Nimshaw and Ashenfelter.)

FORDYCE: If you'd just fill these out, please. We're trying to accumulate data on everybody who uses the data bank so we can eventually tie it all in with something or other.

(Nimshaw studies the section of his card dealing with maximum fines and imprisonment for giving false information, while Ashenfelter skips over the hard part and goes directly to the multiple-choice questions.)

FORDYCE: And try to be as specific as you can about religious beliefs and your affiliation with subversive groups. We're beginning to think there's more to this business of Quakers' denying they belong to the Minutemen than meets the eye.

(Nimshaw and Ashenfelter squirm uneasily as they sense the implication. Ashenfelter hurriedly changes his answer regarding prayer in public schools from "undecided" to "not necessarily" as Nimshaw perjures himself by listing the principal activity at the Forest Hills Tennis Club as tennis. Meantime, Gippard has rejoined the group, carrying four rolls of computer tape carefully stacked in no particular sequence.)

GIPPARD: I know I'm on to something here, Fordyce, but I'm

not sure what to make of it. Surveillance reports on kosher poultry dealers indicate that most of them don't even show up for work on Saturday. And that timing correlates with an unexplained increase in activity at golf courses near key military installations. But the big thing is that drunken drivers tend to get nabbed most often on Saturday night, and that's exactly when organized groups are endangering national security by deliberately staying up late with their lights turned on to overload public power plants.

FORDYCE: (*whistles softly in amazement*): We're really going to catch a covey of them in this net. How'd you happen to stumble across it all?

GIPPARD: Well, it seemed pretty innocent at first. This clown from Indian Affairs just asked me to dig up what I could so he'd have some excuse for exterminating the Jews.

(*Ashenfelter emits a burbling throat noise as an apparent prelude to something more coherent, but he is quickly shushed.*)

GIPPARD: But you know how one correlation always leads to another. Now we've got a grizzly by the tail, Fordyce, and I can see "organized conspiracy" written all over it.

FORDYCE: Beyond question. And somewhere among those 192 million dossiers is the ID number of the Mister Big we're after. Do the machines compute a cause-and-effect relationship that might help narrow things down?

GIPPARD: Well, frankly, the computers have gotten into a pretty nasty argument among themselves over that. Most of them see how golf could lead to drunken driving. But the one that's programmed to chart moral decay and leisure time fun is pretty sure that drunken driving causes golf.

(*Nimshaw glances up from the job of filling out his registry card.*)

NIMSHAW: That's the most ridiculous thing I ever heard in my life.

FORDYCE: (*with forced restraint*): General, would you please stick to whatever people like you are supposed to know about and leave computer-finding interpretation to analysts who are trained for the job?

(*Nimshaw starts to reply, but then recalls the fate of a fellow officer who was broken to corporal for insubordination. He meekly resumes pondering question No. 153, unable to decide whether admitting or denying the purchase of Girl Scout cookies will weigh most heavily against him in years to come.)*

FORDYCE: Any other cause-and-effect computations that we ought to consider in depth, Gipp?

GIPPARD: Not really. Of course, Number 327's been out of step with the others ever since it had that circuitry trouble. It just keeps saying, "Malcolm W. Biggs causes kosher poultry." Types out the same damned thing over and over: "Malcolm W. Biggs causes kosher poultry."

FORDYCE: Who's Malcolm W. Biggs?

GIPPARD: I think he was a juror at one of the Jimmy Hoffa trials. Number 327 was running a check on him when the circuits blew, and it's had kind of an obsession about him ever since.

FORDYCE: Mmmm. Well, personally, I've never paid much attention to the opinions of paranoids. They can get your thinking as screwed up as theirs is.

(Fordyce notices that Ashenfelter is making an erasure on his card to change the data regarding his shoe size from 9½C to something less likely to pinch across the instep.)

FORDYCE *(shrieks at Ashenfelter)*: What do you think you're doing there? You're trying to hide something from me. I've met your kind before.

(Ahenfelter wearily goes bank to a 9½C, even though they make his feet hurt, and Fordyce reacts with a look of smug satisfaction.)

GIPPARD: Maybe if I fed this junk back into the machine, it could name some people who fit the pattern.

FORDYCE: Why don't you just reprocess the computations in an effort to gain individualized data that correlates?

(Gippard stares thoughtfully at Fordyce for a long moment and then exits to nail the ringleaders through incriminating association with the key words "drunk," "poultry," "golf," and "kilowatt.")

NIMSHAW: I think maybe I'd better come back sometime when you're not so busy.